SIDE by SIDE Plus

BOOK 2B

Life Skills, Standards, & Test Prep

Steven J. Molinsky • Bill Blis

Illustrated by Richard E. Hill

Dedicated to Tina Carver with gratitude for her inspiration and contribution to the development of the original *Side by Side* program.

Steven J. Molinsky
Bill Bliss

Side by Side Plus, Book 2B

Pearson Education, 10 Bank Street, White Plains, NY 10606

Editorial director: *Pam Fishman*
Vice president, director of design and production: *Rhea Banker*
Director of electronic production: *Aliza Greenblatt*
Director of manufacturing: *Patrice Fraccio*
Senior manufacturing manager: *Edith Pullman*
Director of marketing: *Oliva Fernandez*
Production editor: *Diane Cipollone*
Senior digital layout specialists: *Wendy Wolf; Warren Fischbach; Lisa Ghiozzi*
Text design: *Wanda España, Wee Design Group; Wendy Wolf*
Cover design: *Wanda España, Wee Design Group; Warren Fischbach*
Realia creation: *Wendy Wolf; Warren Fischbach*
Image archivist: *Paula Williams*
Illustrations: *Richard E. Hill*
Principal photographer: *Paul I. Tañedo*
Contributing authors: *Laura English, Elizabeth Handley, Meredith Westfall*
Manager, visual research: *Beth Brenzel*
Image permission coordinator: *Angelique Sharps*
Photo researcher: *Teri Stratford*

Additional photos: p.70b (*first*) Harris Shiffman/Shutterstock, (*second*) Harris Shiffman/Shutterstock, (*fifth*) Stephen Finn/Shutterstock; p.70c Ryan McVay/Getty Images; p.81 SuperStock, Inc.; p.82 (*top, left*) ©Steve Raymer/CORBIS, (*top, right*) ©Martin Rogers/CORBIS, (*center, left*) S. Noorani/Woodfin Camp & Associates, (*right, center*) Vo-Trung Dung/Woodfin Camp & Associates, (*bottom, left*) Capital Features/The Image Works, (*bottom, right*) Ranald Mackechnie/Stone; p.102a (*1st row, right*) Michael Brown/Getty Images; p.103 (*center*) Tom McCarthy/PhotoEdit, (*left*) Owen Franken/Stock Boston, (*right*) Jose Pelaez/The Stock Market; p.104 (*top*) Seth Resnick/Stock Boston, (*center*) Stephanie Maze/Corbis, (*bottom*) Bob Daemmrich/The Image Works; p.137 Robert Brenner/PhotoEdit, p.138 (*top*) Jeff Greenberg/International Stock Photography Ltd., (*center*) Bill Bachmann/PhotoEdit, (*bottom*) Fritz Hoffmann/The Image Works.

Pearson Longman on the Web
PearsonLongman.com offers online resources for teachers and students.
Access our Companion Websites, our online catalog, and our local offices around the world.
Visit us at pearsonlongman.com.

ISBN 978-0-13-209013-1; 0-13-209013-9

Printed in the United States of America
1 2 3 4 5 6 7 8 9 10 – QWD – 12 11 10 09 08

CONTENTS

Red type indicates new standards-based lessons.

Dear Friends,

Welcome to ***Side by Side Plus*** a special edition for adult learners that offers an integrated standards-based and grammar-based approach to language learning!

Flexible Language Proficiency *Plus* Life Skills

The core mission of *Side by Side Plus* is to build students general language proficiency so they can use English flexibly to meet their varied needs, life circumstances, and goals. We strongly believe that language teachers need to preserve their role as true teachers of language even as we fill our lesson plans with required life-skill content and prepare students for standardized tests. Our program helps you accomplish this through a research-based grammatical sequence and communicative approach in which basic language lessons in each unit lead to standards-based lessons focused on students life-skill roles in the community, family, school, and at work.

Keys to Promoting Student Persistence and Success

Student-Centered Learning The core methodology of *Side by Side Plus* is the guided conversation a brief, structured dialog that students practice in pairs and then use as a framework to create new conversations. Through this practice, students work together to develop their language skills side by side. They are not dependent on the teacher for all instruction, and they know how to learn from each other. This student-centered methodology and the text s easy-to-use format enable students to study outside of class with any speaking partner a family member, a friend or neighbor, a tutor, or a co-worker, even if that person is also an English language learner. If students need to attend class intermittently or stop out for a while, they have the skills and text material to continue learning on their own.

Meaningful Instruction Relevant to Students' Lives Throughout the instructional program, civics topics and tasks connect students to their community, personalization questions apply lesson content to students life situations, and critical-thinking activities build a community of learners who problem-solve together and share solutions.

Extending Learning Outside the Classroom The magazine-style Gazette sections in *Side by Side Plus* provide motivating material for students to use at home. Feature articles, vocabulary enrichment, and other activities reinforce classroom instruction through high-interest material that students are motivated to use outside of class. A bonus Audio CD offers entertaining radio program-style recordings of key Gazette activities. (See the inside back cover for a description of other media materials and software designed to extend learning through self-study.)

Sufficient Practice + Frequent Assessment = Success Students need to experience success as language learners. While other programs cover many learning objectives, *Side by Side Plus* offers students carefully-sequenced intensive practice that promotes mastery and the successful application of language skills to daily life. Students can observe their achievement milestones through the program s frequent assessments, including check-up tests and skills checklists in the text and achievement tests in the accompanying workbook.

The "Fun Factor" We believe that language instruction is most powerful when it is joyful. There is magic in the power of humor, fun, games, and music to encourage students to take risks with their emerging language, to play with it, and to allow their personalities to shine through as their language skills increase. We incorporate these elements into our program to motivate students to persist in their language learning not only because they need it, but also because they enjoy it.

Multilevel Instruction *Side by Side Plus* provides exceptional resources to support multilevel instruction. The Teacher s Guide includes step-by-step instructions for preparing below-level and at-level students for each lesson and hundreds of multilevel activities for all students, including those above-level. The accompanying Multilevel Activity & Achievement Test Book and CD-ROM offer an array of reproducible multilevel worksheets and activities.

We hope your students enjoy using *Side by Side Plus.* We are confident that these resources will help them persist and succeed through a language learning experience that is effective . . . relevant to their lives . . . and fun!

Steven J. Molinsky
Bill Bliss

Guide to Life Skills, Standards, & Test Prep Features

Side by Side has helped over 25 million students worldwide persist and succeed as language learners. Now, in this special edition for adult learners in standards-based programs, ***Side by Side Plus*** builds students' general language proficiency *and* helps them apply these skills for success meeting the needs of daily life and work.

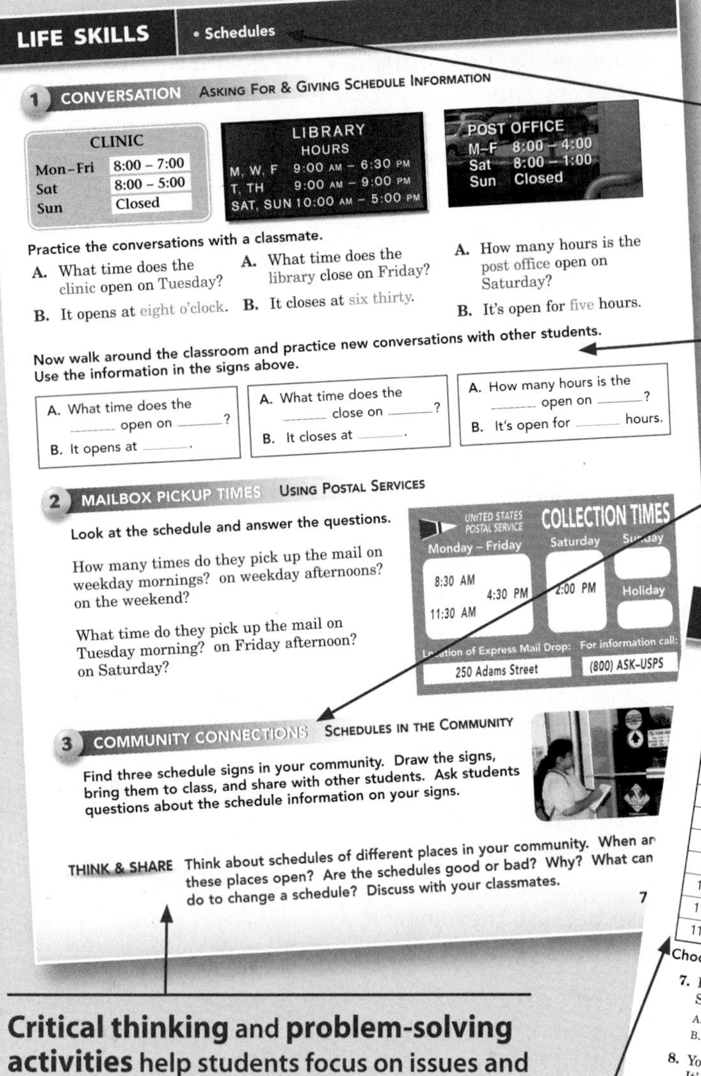

LIFE SKILLS • Schedules

1 CONVERSATION Asking For & Giving Schedule Information

CLINIC
Mon–Fri 8:00 – 7:00
Sat 8:00 – 5:00
Sun Closed
LIBRARY
HOURS
M, W, F 9:00 AM – 6:30 PM
T, TH 9:00 AM – 9:00 PM
SAT, SUN 10:00 AM – 5:00 PM
POST OFFICE
M–F 8:00 – 4:00
Sat 8:00 – 1:00
Sun Closed

Practice the conversations with a classmate.

A. What time does the clinic open on Tuesday?
B. It opens at eight o'clock.

A. What time does the library close on Friday?
B. It closes at six thirty.

A. How many hours is the post office open on Saturday?
B. It's open for five hours.

Now walk around the classroom and practice new conversations with other students. Use the information in the signs above.

A. What time does the ______ open on ______?
B. It opens at ______.

A. What time does the ______ close on ______?
B. It closes at ______.

A. How many hours is the ______ open on ______?
B. It's open for ______ hours.

2 MAILBOX PICKUP TIMES Using Postal Services

Look at the schedule and answer the questions.

How many times do they pick up the mail on weekday mornings? on weekday afternoons? on the weekend?

What time do they pick up the mail on Tuesday morning? on Friday afternoon? on Saturday?

UNITED STATES POSTAL SERVICE
COLLECTION TIMES
Monday – Friday
Saturday
Sunday
8:30 AM
11:30 AM
4:30 PM
2:00 PM
Holiday
Location of Express Mail Drop:
250 Adams Street
For information call:
(800) ASK-USPS

3 COMMUNITY CONNECTIONS Schedules in the Community

Find three schedule signs in your community. Draw the signs, bring them to class, and share with other students. Ask students questions about the schedule information on your signs.

THINK & SHARE Think about schedules of different places in your community. When ar[e] these places open? Are the schedules good or bad? Why? What can [...] do to change a schedule? Discuss with your classmates.

7

Standards-based lessons at the end of every unit apply students' language learning to their life-skill roles in the community, family, school, and at work. Students develop the key competencies included in CASAS, BEST Plus, EFF, SCANS, Model Standards, and other major state and local curriculum frameworks and assessment systems.

Real-life conversation practice in authentic life-skill situations gets students talking through interactive pair work. **Extensive illustrations and photographs** provide clear contexts and support vocabulary learning.

Community tasks introduce basic civics topics related to community life and help students connect to community information and services.

Critical thinking and **problem-solving activities** help students focus on issues and problems and share ideas and solutions.

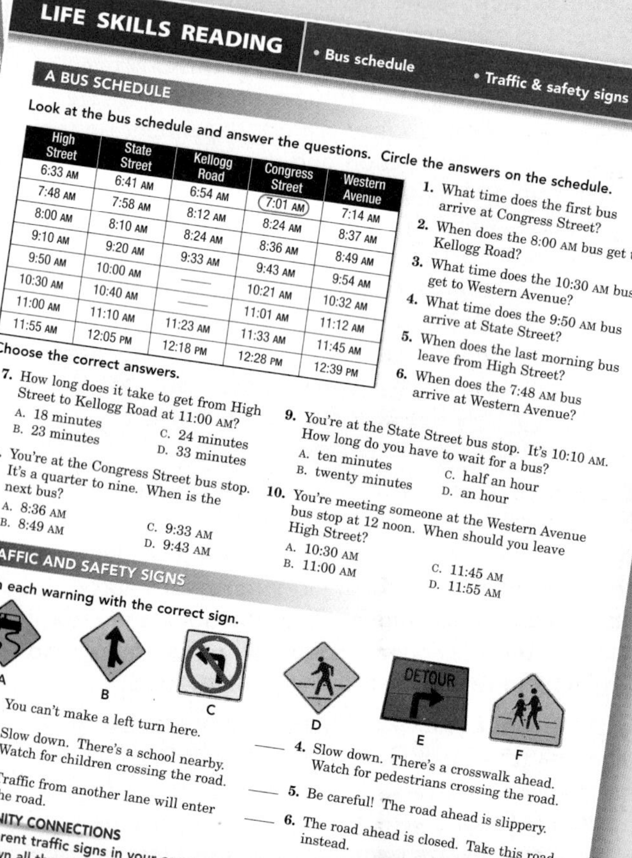

LIFE SKILLS READING • Bus schedule • Traffic & safety signs

A BUS SCHEDULE

Look at the bus schedule and answer the questions. Circle the answers on the schedule.

High Street	State Street	Kellogg Road	Congress Street	Western Avenue
6:33 AM	6:41 AM	6:54 AM	7:01 AM	7:14 AM
7:48 AM	7:58 AM	8:12 AM	8:24 AM	8:37 AM
8:00 AM	8:10 AM	8:24 AM	8:36 AM	8:49 AM
9:10 AM	9:20 AM	9:33 AM	9:43 AM	9:54 AM
9:50 AM	10:00 AM	—	10:21 AM	10:32 AM
10:30 AM	10:40 AM	—	11:01 AM	11:12 AM
11:00 AM	11:10 AM	11:23 AM	11:33 AM	11:45 AM
11:55 AM	12:05 PM	12:18 PM	12:28 PM	12:39 PM

1. What time does the first bus arrive at Congress Street?
2. When does the 8:00 AM bus get to Kellogg Road?
3. What time does the 10:30 AM bus get to Western Avenue?
4. What time does the 9:50 AM bus arrive at State Street?
5. When does the last morning bus leave from High Street?
6. When does the 7:48 AM bus arrive at Western Avenue?

Choose the correct answers.

7. How long does it take to get from High Street to Kellogg Road at 11:00 AM?
   A. 18 minutes B. 23 minutes C. 24 minutes D. 33 minutes
8. You're at the Congress Street bus stop. It's a quarter to nine. When is the next bus?
   A. 8:36 AM B. 8:49 AM C. 9:33 AM D. 9:43 AM
9. You're at the State Street bus stop. It's 10:10 AM. How long do you have to wait for a bus?
   A. ten minutes B. twenty minutes C. half an hour D. an hour
10. You're meeting someone at the Western Avenue bus stop at 12 noon. When should you leave High Street?
   A. 10:30 AM B. 11:00 AM C. 11:45 AM D. 11:55 AM

TRAFFIC AND SAFETY SIGNS

Match each warning with the correct sign.

___ 1. You can't make a left turn here.
___ 2. Slow down. There's a school nearby. Watch for children crossing the road.
___ 3. Traffic from another lane will enter the road.
___ 4. Slow down. There's a crosswalk ahead. Watch for pedestrians crossing the road.
___ 5. Be careful! The road ahead is slippery.
___ 6. The road ahead is closed. Take this road instead.

COMMUNITY CONNECTIONS

Find different traffic signs in your community and draw them. Write down all the words and symbols on the signs. Bring your signs to class, and compare signs with other students.

70b

Realia-based reading activities include schedules, product labels, advertisements, store receipts, menus, ATM screens, help wanted ads, and telephone directories.

Life skills writing activities include signs, forms, phone messages, job applications, invitations, checks, recipes, notes to a child's teacher, and letters to the editor.

NARRATIVE READING • Safe driving practices

Safe Driving

More than 3.5 million people get hurt in car accidents in the United States each year. Here are some things you can do so that you and your passengers are safe.

Always wear a seat belt. Also, make sure that all the passengers in your car wear their seat belts. Children under the age of five should ride in child safety seats that you attach to the back seat of the car. The center back seat is the safest.

Many accidents happen when cars are in bad condition. Take good care of your car. Check the brakes every week to be sure that you can stop the car when you need to. Keep the windshield clean so you can see the road ahead. Be sure the windshield wipers work in the rain.

Be a careful driver. Pay attention to traffic signs, road conditions, and other drivers. Look before you make a turn or change lanes on the highway. Don't "tailgate"—don't stay too close to the car in front of you. The driver might stop without warning. Be especially careful when the weather is bad. Slow down and use your headlights in the rain, snow, and fog. Pay attention to the speed limit. When the speed limit is sixty miles an hour, that's the fastest you should drive. On the other hand, don't be a slow driver. Slow drivers can cause accidents.

You can't pay attention to the road when you're tired or busy doing too many things. Don't eat, drink, or talk on your cell phone while you're driving. Don't take any medicine that can make you sleepy before you drive. The label on such medicine usually has the warning "May cause drowsiness." Remember, other drivers are not always as careful as you are. Be prepared for their mistakes. If you are in an accident, the police will ask to see your papers. Always have your license, car registration, and insurance card with you to show to the police.

1. The best place for a child safety seat is ____.
   A. in the front seat
   B. in the back seat next to the door
   C. in the center back seat
   D. next to the driver
2. According to this article, drivers should ____.
   A. use headlights when it's foggy
   B. always drive sixty miles per hour
   C. ride in safety seats
   D. make mistakes
3. According to this article, drivers should NOT ____.
   A. be prepared for other drivers' mistakes
   B. look before changing lanes
   C. use their windshield wipers in the rain
   D. use a cell phone while they're driving
4. A driver who *tailgates* ____.
   A. is a slow driver
   B. drives too close to the car ahead
   C. stops without warning
   D. is a careful driver
5. We can infer that *the windshield* in paragraph 3 ____.
   A. stops the car
   B. cleans the car
   C. is in the back of the car
   D. is in the front of the car
6. *May cause drowsiness* means the medicine ____.
   A. is old
   B. is bad for you
   C. might make you tired
   D. might make you nervous

Narrative reading passages offer practice with simple newspaper and magazine articles on topics such as safe driving practices, cross-cultural expectations, the education system, and nutrition. Reading tips highlight key concepts and skills such as differentiating facts and inferences and recognizing signal words.

Reading comprehension exercises in multiple-choice formats help students prepare for the reading section of standardized tests.

ASSESSMENT • Check-up test • Self-evaluation checklists

Choose the correct answer.

1. I go to the ____ on Main Street to wash my shirts.
   A. shopping mall
   B. department store
   C. hardware store
   D. laundromat
2. They bake wonderful pies and cakes at the ____ down the street.
   A. bank
   B. bakery
   C. barber shop
   D. flower shop
3. I got off the bus at the wrong ____.
   A. stop
   B. map
   C. bus
   D. directions
4. We don't want to be late for the plane. What's the fastest way to get to the ____?
   A. train station
   B. airport
   C. bus station
   D. gas station
5. Can you ____ a good department store in a convenient location?
   A. tell me how
   B. directions
   C. how to get there
   D. recommend
6. What ____ does the clinic close on Monday?
   A. hours
   B. schedule
   C. time
   D. schedule sign
7. When you drive, you should always ____.
   A. ride in a child safety seat
   B. wear a seat belt
   C. tailgate
   D. be a slow driver
8. When you drive, don't ____.
   A. drive and talk on your cell phone
   B. use your headlights in the fog
   C. look before you change lanes
   D. pay attention to the speed limit

Look at the bus schedule. Choose the correct answer.

9. You're at the Lake Street bus stop. It's half past seven. The next bus is at ____.
   A. 6:15 AM
   B. 7:10 AM
   C. 7:55 AM
   D. 8:30 AM
10. You're at the Main Street bus stop. It's a quarter after eight. You have to wait ____ for the next bus.
   A. 6 minutes
   B. 21 minutes
   C. 8:21
   D. 8:51

Lake St.	First Ave.	Main St.	River Rd.
6:15 AM	6:24 AM	6:36 AM	6:42 AM
7:10 AM	7:21 AM	7:34 AM	7:42 AM
7:55 AM	8:07 AM	8:21 AM	8:29 AM
8:30 AM	8:40 AM	8:51AM	8:58 AM

SKILLS CHECK

Words:
- ☐ airport
- ☐ bakery
- ☐ bank
- ☐ barber shop
- ☐ baseball stadium
- ☐ book store
- ☐ bus station
- ☐ cafeteria
- ☐ church
- ☐ clinic
- ☐ concert hall
- ☐ courthouse
- ☐ department store
- ☐ drug store
- ☐ fire station
- ☐ flower shop
- ☐ gas station
- ☐ hardware store
- ☐ high school
- ☐ hospital
- ☐ hotel
- ☐ ice cream shop
- ☐ laundromat
- ☐ library
- ☐ motel
- ☐ museum
- ☐ park
- ☐ parking garage
- ☐ parking lot
- ☐ pet shop
- ☐ playground
- ☐ police station
- ☐ post office
- ☐ restaurant
- ☐ shoe store
- ☐ shopping mall
- ☐ supermarket
- ☐ toy store
- ☐ train station
- ☐ university
- ☐ zoo
- ☐ back seat
- ☐ brakes
- ☐ child safety seat
- ☐ headlights
- ☐ passenger
- ☐ road conditions
- ☐ seat belt
- ☐ speed limit
- ☐ tailgate
- ☐ traffic sign
- ☐ windshield
- ☐ windshield wipers

I can ask & answer:
- ☐ Can you tell me/Could you please tell me/ Would you please tell me how to get *there*?
- ☐ What's the quickest/easiest way to get to the *bank*?
- ☐ What time does the *clinic* open/close on *Tuesday*?

I can read:
- ☐ schedule information on signs
- ☐ a bus schedule
- ☐ traffic & safety signs

I can:
- ☐ draw a map and write directions

I can write about:
- ☐ ways I get to places in my community

70d

Check-up tests allow a quick assessment of student achievement and help prepare students for the kinds of test items found on standardized tests.

More complete **Achievement Tests** for each unit, including listening test items, are available as reproducible masters and printable disk files in the Teacher's Guide with Multilevel Activity & Achievement Test Book and CD-ROM. They are also available in the companion Activity & Test Prep Workbook.

Vocabulary checklists and **language skill checklists** help students review words they have learned, keep track of the skills they are developing, and identify vocabulary and skills they need to continue to work on. These lists promote student persistence as students assess their own skills and check off all the ways they are succeeding as language learners.

Scope and Sequence

ALL-SKILLS COMMUNICATION: LISTENING, SPEAKING, READING, WRITING

Unit	Topics, Vocabulary, & Math	Grammar	Functional Communication	Listening & Pronunciation	Writing
7	• Getting around town • Places in the community • Public transportation • Following a map or diagram indicating directions to a destination • Schedules of building hours • Bus schedules • Traffic & safety signs • Safe driving practices	• Imperatives • Directions	• Giving & following instructions • Asking for repetition • Asking for & giving recommendations	• Listening for specific information in directions • Listening to make deductions about the location of conversations • Pronouncing *could you* & *would you*	• Drawing a map & writing directions to your home • Writing about how to get to different places in the community • Drawing schedule signs found in the community • Drawing traffic signs found in the community
8	• Describing people's actions • Occupations • Describing plans & intentions • Consequences of actions • Job interview • Stating skills & work experience • Asking for permission at work • Help wanted ads • Reading a paycheck & pay stub • Employee accident report	• Adverbs • Comparative of adverbs • Agent nouns • If-clauses	• Expressing an opinion • Expressing agreement • Asking for & giving feedback about job performance • Asking about & giving information about future plans • Giving & receiving advice	• Listening to determine the correct consequences of actions • Pronouncing contrastive stress	• Writing about something you want to do and the consequences of doing it • Filling out a job application form • Filling out an employee accident report form
Gazette	• Tips for a successful job interview • Occupations • Culture concept: Men's & women's jobs in different countries	• Adverbs • Agent nouns	• Interpreting advice • Describing self	• Listening to & interpreting announcements at a workplace correctly	• Writing an e-mail or instant message to tell about your skills & activities
9	• Describing ongoing past activities • Describing an accident • Reporting a home emergency • Emergency preparedness • First-aid instructions • Warning labels on household products • Safety procedures: Earthquakes & hurricanes	• Past continuous tense • Reflexive pronouns • While-clauses	• Asking about & giving information about past events • Expressing concern about someone • Expressing sympathy • Reacting to bad news • Describing a sequence of events	• Listening to make deductions about the context of conversations • Pronouncing *did* & *was*	• Writing about preference for doing things alone or with other people
10	• Expressing past & future ability • Expressing past & future obligation • Giving an excuse • Renting an apartment • Housing ads • Reading a floor plan • Requesting maintenance & repairs • Building rules & regulations	• Could • Be able to • Have got to • Too + adjective	• Asking and telling about ability to do things • Expressing obligation • Describing physical states & emotions	• Listening for correct situation or context • Pronouncing *have to* & *have got to*	• Writing about a time you were frustrated, disappointed, or upset • Writing about an apartment or home • Drawing a floor plan • Writing a housing ad

CORRELATION and PLACEMENT KEY

Side by Side Plus 2 correlates with these standards-based curriculum levels and assessment system score ranges.

For correlation keys to other major state and local curriculum frameworks, please visit:
www.pearsonlongman.com/sidebysideplus

NRS (National Reporting System) Educational Functioning Level	High Beginning
SPL (Student Performance Level)	3
CASAS (Comprehensive Adult Student Assessment System)	191–200
BEST Plus (Basic English Skills Test)	418–438
BEST Oral Interview	29–41
BEST Literacy	36–46

Life Skills, Civics, Test Preparation, Curriculum Standards and Frameworks

Life Skills, Civics, & Test Preparation	EFF	SCANS/Employment Competencies	CASAS	LAUSD	Florida*
• Interpreting schedules • Locating places on a map • Compass directions • Reading a bus schedule • Traffic & safety signs & symbols • Police commands & traffic signs • Postal services • Simple written directions • Drawing a map • Safe driving practices	• Identify community resources • Seek & receive assistance • Give direction • Understand, interpret, & work with numbers & symbolic information • Gather, analyze, & use information • Reflect & evaluate • Provide for family members' safety & physical needs	• Identify resources • Communicate information • See things in the mind's eye (Interpret a simple route map; Draw a simple route map; Interpret symbols on signs) • Acquire & evaluate information • Problem solving	0.1.2, 1.1.4, 1.9.1, 2.2.1, 2.2.2, 2.4.2, 2.4.4, 2.5.4, 2.6.1, 2.6.2, 6.6.4	8a, 22, 23, 24, 31, 41, 42	3.02.02, 3.08.02, 3.09.02, 3.09.03, 3.09.04, 3.09.05, 3.09.06, 3.12.01, 3.12.02, 3.15.08
• Help wanted ads (with abbreviations) • Job interview questions about skills & work history • Describing a work schedule • Calling in sick & late • Requesting a schedule change • Employee accident reports • Reading a paycheck & pay stub • Nonverbal behavior at the job interview • Identifying ways to improve performance at work & at school	• Cooperate with others • Work together • Seek input from others • Guide & support others • Work within the big picture • Create goals • Reflect & evaluate • Gather, analyze, & use information • Work together	• Participate as a member of a team • Self-management: Monitor progress • Responsibility • Decision making • Self-esteem • Identify human resources (occupations; work skills) • Problem solving • Acquire & evaluate information • Participate as a member of a team	0.1.3, 0.2.1, 0.2.2, 4.1.2, 4.1.3, 4.1.5, 4.1.6, 4.1.7, 4.2.1, 4.3.4, 4.4.1, 4.4.3, 4.6.5	8, 51, 52, 53, 54, 55, 56, 57	3.01.01, 3.01.02, 3.01.03, 3.01.05, 3.01.06, 3.02.01, 3.02.02, 3.02.03, 3.02.04, 3.05.01, 3.16.08
• Identifying appropriate job interview behaviors, including dress, promptness, eye contact, speaking style, honesty, & confidence • Identifying occupations • Interpreting announcements over a workplace P.A. system	• Analyze & use information • Develop & express sense of self • Interact in a way that is friendly & courteous • Respect others & value diversity	• Acquire & evaluate information • Self-esteem • Integrity/Honesty • Sociability • Work with cultural diversity	0.2.1, 4.1.5, 4.1.6, 4.1.7	53, 54	3.01.01, 3.01.02, 3.01.06, 3.02.02, 3.02.03, 3.03.02, 3.05.02, 3.05.03, 3.05.04, 3.15.12, 3.16.08
• Calling 911 • First-aid instructions • Describing a suspect's physical characteristics to the police • Warning labels on household products • Interpreting emergency procedures on safety posters • Learning skills: Categorizing words, Word sets	• Interact in a way that is friendly • Identify problems • Develop & express sense of self • Identify resources • Provide for family members' safety & physical needs • Work together • Reflect & evaluate	• Sociability • Self-esteem • Communicate information • Participate as a member of a team • Problem solving	0.1.2, 0.1.4, 0.2.2, 0.2.4, 2.1.2, 3.4.1, 3.4.2, 3.4.3, 7.2.3	3, 6, 7a, 7b, 10b, 20, 48, 49, 50, 64	3.05.01, 3.06.01, 3.10.01, 3.10.02, 3.13.01, 3.14.01, 3.15.07, 3.16.02
• Housing ads (with abbreviations) • Inquiring about rentals • Describing maintenance & repairs needed in a rental unit • Interpreting a floor plan/diagram • Interpreting an apartment building regulations notice	• Interact in a way that is tactful • Identify supportive friendships • Reflect & evaluate • Work together • Gather, analyze, & use information • Exercise rights & responsibilities	• Sociability • Self-esteem • Participate as a member of a team • Acquire & evaluate information • See things in the mind's eye (Interpret and draw diagrams)	0.1.2, 0.1.4, 1.4.2, 1.4.7, 7.4.1	7b, 9b, 10a, 37, 38, 39, 62	3.11.04, 3.15.08, 3.16.03

EFF: Equipped for the Future (Content standards, Common activities, & Key activities for Citizen/Community Member, Worker, & Parent/Family role maps; EFF Communication and Reflection/Evaluation skills are covered in every unit)
SCANS: Secretary's Commission on Achieving Necessary Skills (U.S. Department of Labor)
CASAS: Comprehensive Adult Student Assessment System
LAUSD: Los Angeles Unified School District (ESL Beginning High content standards)
Florida: Adult ESOL High Beginning Standardized Syllabi

(*Florida benchmarks 3.15.01, 3.15.02, 3.15,03, 3.15.04, 3.15.05, 3.15.11, 3.15.13, 3.16.01, 3.16.02, 3.16.05, 3.16.06, 3.16.07, 3.16.09, 3.17.01, 3.17.02, and 3.17.03 are covered in every unit.)

Scope and Sequence

All-Skills Communication: Listening, Speaking, Reading, Writing

Unit	Topics, Vocabulary, & Math	Grammar	Functional Communication	Listening & Pronunciation	Writing
Gazette	• Families & time • Interpreting a table with number facts • Home appliances • Culture concept: Child-care around the world	• Tense review • Have to / Have got to	• Describing daily life & customs	• Listening to messages on a telephone answering machine	• Writing an e-mail or instant message to tell about activities and occurrences during the week
11	• Medical examinations • Medical advice • Health • Foods • Nutrition • Home remedies • Making a doctor appointment • Calling in sick • Reporting absence from school • Medicine labels • Medicine safety tips • Nutrition & recipes	• Past tense review • Count/Non-count noun review • Must • Mustn't vs. Don't have to • Must vs. Should	• Asking for & giving advice • Describing a future sequence of events • Describing a past sequence of events • Expressing concern	• Listening for key words to determine subject matter of conversations • Pronouncing *must* & *mustn't*	• Making a list of healthy and unhealthy foods • Writing about rules in life • Writing a note to a teacher to explain a child's absence • Writing about favorite healthy foods • Writing a recipe • Filling out a medical history form
12	• Describing future activities • Expressing time & duration • Making plans by telephone • Handling wrong-number calls • Leaving & taking phone messages • Telephone directory: White pages, government pages, & yellow pages • Using a telephone response system	• Future continuous tense • Time expressions	• Asking and telling about future plans & activities • Calling people on the telephone • Borrowing & returning items	• Listening to messages on a telephone answering machine • Pronouncing contractions with *will*	• Writing about a family holiday celebration • Writing telephone messages
13	• Offering help • Indicating ownership • Household problems • Using the telephone to request household maintenance and repairs • Reading a rental agreement • Tenants' rights • Car trouble • Friends	• Some/Any • Pronoun review • Verb tense review	• Offering help • Asking & telling about past events • Asking for & giving advice • Describing problems	• Listening for correct pronouns in conversations • Listening to make deductions about the subject of conversations • Pronouncing deleted *h*	• Writing about relying on friends for help • Writing about a very good friend • Filling out an apartment maintenance/repair request form
Gazette	• Communities—urban, suburban, & rural • Interpreting a bar graph with population data in millions • Household repair people • Culture concept: Where friends gather in different countries around the world	• Present tense review • Future tense review	• Describing community life • Describing future events	• Listening to telephone conversations & answering machine messages to make deductions about the subject of conversations	• Writing an e-mail or instant message to tell about a future family celebration

Life Skills, Civics, Test Preparation, Curriculum Standards and Frameworks

Life Skills, Civics, & Test Preparation	EFF	SCANS/Employment Competencies	CASAS	LAUSD	Florida*
• Interpreting a narrative reading about daily life & customs • Interpreting statistical facts in a table • Interpreting telephone messages on an answering machine	• Analyze information • Identify supportive family relationships • Meet family needs & responsibilities • Understand, interpret, & work with numbers • Respect others & value diversity • Use technology & other tools to accomplish goals	• Acquire & evaluate information • Work with cultural diversity • Work with technology (telephone answering device)	0.1.2, 0.2.4, 2.1.7, 7.4.1	7a, 18, 62	3.06.02, 3.14.03, 3.15.08, 3.15.12, 3.16.02
• Identifying parts of the face & body • Common symptoms • Calling to report an absence • Making a doctor appointment • Procedures during a medical exam • Common prescription & non-prescription medicines • Interpreting medicine label dosages & instructions • A note to the teacher explaining a child's absence • Learning skill: Categorizing foods & nutrients	• Seek guidance & support from others • Guide & support others • Meet family needs & responsibilities • Work together	• Acquire & evaluate information • Self-management • Understand a social system • Participate as a member of a team	0.1.2, 2.5.5, 3.1.1, 3.1.2, 3.2.1, 3.3.1, 3.3.2, 3.3.3, 4.4.1	16, 43, 44, 45, 46, 47, 55	3.07.01, 3.07.03, 3.07.04, 3.07.05, 3.14.04, 3.16.02, 3.16.06
• Life cycle—stages & events • Holidays • Beginning & ending a telephone conversation • Using the telephone directory: White pages, government pages, & yellow pages • Phone messages • Recorded telephone information • Fahrenheit & Celsius temperatures	• Interact in a way that is friendly & courteous • Manage resources: Allocate time • Create a vision for the future • Identify a strong sense of family • Gather information • Identify community resources • Use technology	• Identify goal-relevant activities • Allocate time • Self-esteem • Acquire & evaluate information • Identify resources • Work with technology (recorded telephone announcements; telephone response system)	0.1.4, 0.2.4, 1.1.5, 2.1.1, 2.1.7, 2.1.8, 2.3.2, 7.4.5	7a, 9, 17, 18, 19, 21, 25, 26, 58	3.05.01, 3.06.02, 3.06.03, 3.06.05, 3.12.04, 3.13.01, 3.14.01, 3.16.02
• Household repair problems • Securing household repair services • Interpreting a lease • Tenants' rights & responsibilities • Reading a TV schedule • Recorded telephone instructions • Making a schedule	• Identify problems • Interact in a way that is tactful • Identify supportive friendships • Identify problems • Seek & receive assistance • Reflect & evaluate • Exercise rights & responsibilities	• Participate as a member of a team • Understand a social system (an apartment building & neighbors) • Identify resources • Work with technology (recorded telephone instructions) • Problem solving	1.4.7, 2.1.7, 2.1.8, 2.6.1, 2.6.2	17, 18, 22, 39, 63	3.05.01, 3.06.02, 3.06.05, 3.08.03, 3.11.04, 3.14.01, 3.15.08, 3.16.02
• Interpreting a narrative reading about types of communities • Interpreting statistical facts in a bar graph • Identifying home repair needs & home repair services	• Analyze & use information • Identify community needs & resources • Understand, interpret, & work with numbers & symbolic information • Respect others & value diversity • Use technology & other tools to accomplish goals	• Acquire & evaluate information • Understand a social system (communities) • See things in the mind's eye (Interpret a bar graph) • Work with cultural diversity	0.1.2, 0.2.4, 1.4.7, 7.4.1	7a, 39, 62	3.05.01, 3.15.08, 3.15.12, 3.16.02

Imperatives
Directions

- Getting Around Town
- Public Transportation
- Schedules of Building Hours
- Bus Schedules
- Traffic and Safety Signs
- Safe Driving Practices

Vocabulary Preview

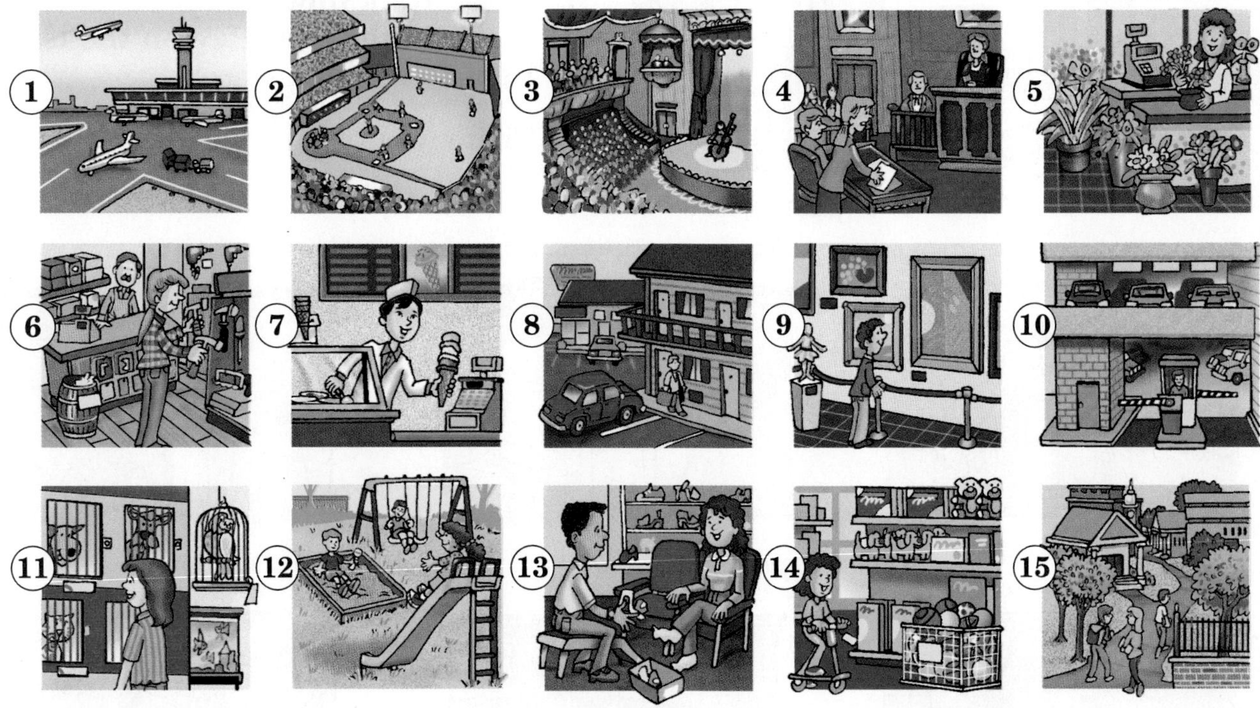

1. airport
2. baseball stadium
3. concert hall
4. courthouse
5. flower shop
6. hardware store
7. ice cream shop
8. motel
9. museum
10. parking garage
11. pet shop
12. playground
13. shoe store
14. toy store
15. university

Can You Tell Me How to Get to . . . ?

walk up walk down	on the right on the left	across from next to between

laundromat?

A. Excuse me. Can you tell me how to get to the laundromat from here?

B. Sure. **Walk up** Main Street and you'll see the laundromat **on the right, across from** the drug store.

A. Thank you.

post office?

A. Excuse me. Can you tell me how to get to the post office from here?

B. Sure. **Walk down** Main Street and you'll see the post office **on the left, next to** the high school.

A. Thank you.

1. *clinic?*

2. *police station?*

3. *drug store?*

4. *library?*

5. *barber shop?*

6. *toy store?*

Could You Please Tell Me How to Get to . . . ?

walk along	on the right on the left	across from next to between

hospital?

A. Excuse me. Could you please tell me how to get to the hospital from here?

B. Sure. **Walk along** Central Avenue and you'll see the hospital **on the left, between** the museum and the park.

A. Thanks.

1. *museum?*

2. *university?*

3. *park?*

4. *hotel?*

5. *parking lot?*

6. *zoo?*

Would You Please Tell Me How to Get to . . . ?

turn left   turn right

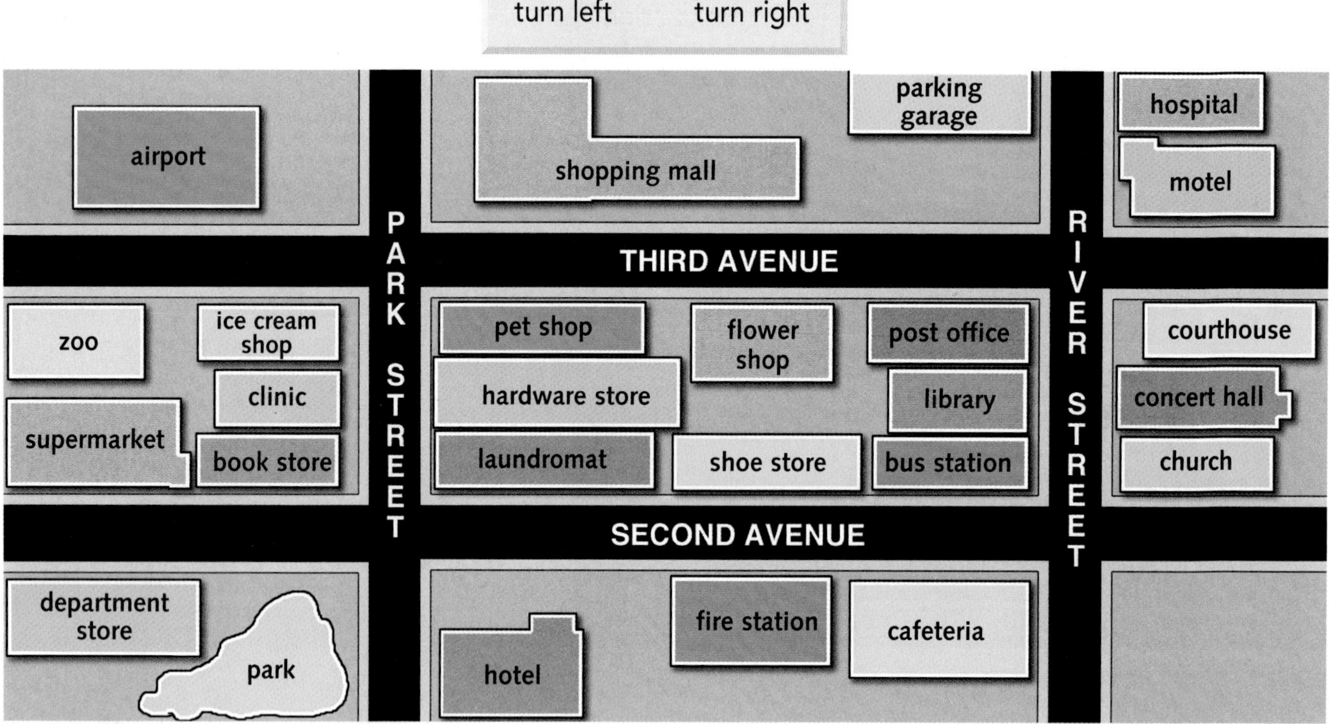

bus station?

A. Excuse me. Would you please tell me how to get to the bus station from here?

B. Certainly. **Walk up** Park Street to Second Avenue and **turn right**. **Walk along** Second Avenue and you'll see the bus station **on the left, across from** the cafeteria.

A. Thanks very much.

concert hall?

A. Excuse me. Would you please tell me how to get to the concert hall from here?

B. Certainly. **Drive along** Second Avenue to River Street and **turn left**. **Drive up** River Street and you'll see the concert hall **on the right, between** the courthouse and the church.

A. Thanks very much.

1. *hospital?*

2. *zoo?*

3. *shoe store?*

4. *laundromat?*

5. *supermarket?*

6. *post office?*

7. *clinic?*

8. *airport?*

9.

How to Say It!

Asking for Repetition

A. I'm sorry. Could you please { repeat that? / say that again? }

B. Sure. *Walk along . . .*

Practice some conversations on this page again. Ask people to repeat the directions.

Take the Main Street Bus

A. Excuse me. What's the quickest way to get to Peter's Pet Shop?

B. **Take** the Main Street bus and **get off** at First Avenue. **Walk up** First Avenue and you'll see Peter's Pet Shop **on the right**.

A. Thank you very much.

B. You're welcome.

A. Excuse me. What's the easiest way to get to Harry's Barber Shop?

B. **Take** the subway and **get off** at Fourth Avenue. **Walk down** Fourth Avenue and you'll see Harry's Barber Shop **on the left**.

A. Thank you very much.

B. You're welcome.

1. What's the fastest way to get to the baseball stadium?

2. What's the best way to get to the library?

3. What's the most direct way to get to the zoo?

4. I'm in a hurry! What's the shortest way to get to the train station?

ROLE PLAY *Can You Tell Me How to Get There?*

A. Can you recommend **a good hotel**?

B. Yes. The Bellview is **a good hotel**. I think it's **one of the best hotels** in town.

A. Can you tell me how to get there?

B. Sure. Take the subway and get off at Brighton Boulevard. You'll see the Bellview at the corner of Brighton Boulevard and Twelfth Street.

A. Thank you very much.

B. You're welcome.

These people are visiting your city. Recommend real places you know and like, and give directions.

Can you recommend a good restaurant?

Can you recommend a big department store?

Can you recommend an interesting tourist sight?

Can you recommend ______________?

READING

HAROLD NEVER GOT THERE!

Dear Students,

Here are directions to my house. I'll see you at the party.

Your English teacher

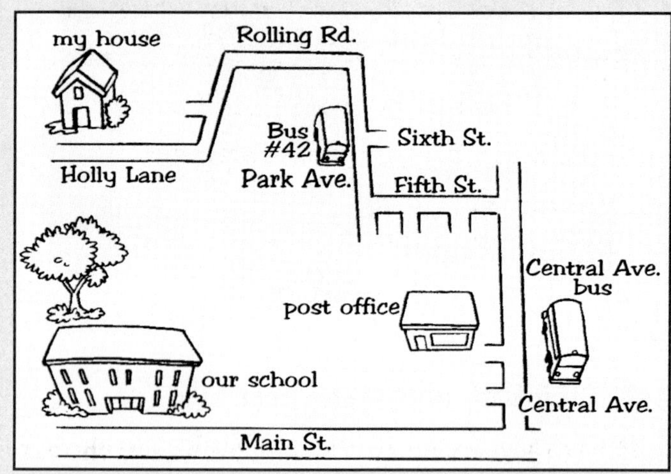

1. From our school, walk along Main St. to Central Ave. and turn left.
2. Walk up Central Ave. 2 blocks, and you'll see a bus stop at the corner, across from the post office.
3. Take the Central Ave. bus and get off at Fifth St.
4. Turn left and walk along Fifth St. 3 blocks to Park Ave. and turn right.
5. Walk up Park Ave. 1 block, and you'll see a bus stop at the corner of Park Ave. and Sixth St.
6. Take Bus #42 and get off at Rolling Rd.
7. Turn left and walk along Rolling Rd. 1 block.
8. Turn left again, and walk 2 blocks to Holly Lane and turn right.
9. Walk along Holly Lane. My house is the last one on the right.

Harold was very disappointed last night. All the other students in his English class went to a party at their teacher's house, but Harold never got there. He followed his teacher's directions, but he made one little mistake.

From their school, he walked along Main Street to Central Avenue and turned left. He walked up Central Avenue two blocks to the bus stop at the corner, across from the post office. He took the Central Avenue bus and got off at Fifth Street. He turned left and walked along Fifth Street three blocks to Park Avenue and turned right. He walked up Park Avenue one block to the bus stop at the corner of Park Avenue and Sixth Street.

He took Bus Number 42, but he got off at the wrong stop. He got off at River Road instead of Rolling Road. He turned left and walked along River Road one block. He turned left again and walked two blocks, turned right, and got completely lost.

Harold was very upset. He really wanted to go to the party last night, and he can't believe he made such a stupid mistake!

✓ READING *CHECK-UP*

TRUE OR FALSE?

1. Harold's English teacher lives on Holly Lane.
2. The Central Avenue bus stops across from the post office.
3. The teacher made one little mistake in the directions.
4. The school is on Main Street.
5. Harold took the wrong bus.
6. Bus Number 42 goes to Rolling Road.
7. Harold got off the bus at Rolling Road.
8. Harold didn't really want to go to the party last night.

WHAT'S THE WORD?

It's very easy to get _____ 1 the zoo from here. Walk up this street _____ 2 the corner and turn right. Walk two blocks and you'll see a bus stop _____ 3 the corner _____ 4 Grove Street and Fourth Avenue. Take the West Side bus and get _____ 5 _____ 6 Park Road. You'll see the zoo _____ 7 the left. It's next _____ 8 the library and across _____ 9 the museum.

LISTENING

WHAT'S THE WORD?

Listen and choose the word you hear.

1. a. right — b. left
2. a. right — b. left
3. a. down — b. up
4. a. along — b. down
5. a. to — b. on
6. a. off — b. of
7. a. on — b. at

WHERE ARE THEY?

Where are these people? Listen and choose the correct place.

1. a. department store — b. laundromat
2. a. pet shop — b. cafeteria
3. a. restaurant — b. library
4. a. hospital — b. hotel
5. a. barber shop — b. supermarket
6. a. parking lot — b. parking garage

IN YOUR OWN WORDS

FOR WRITING AND DISCUSSION

You're going to invite people to your home. Draw a map and write directions to help them get there. (Give them directions from your school.)

PRONUNCIATION *Could you & Would you*

Listen. Then say it.

Could you please tell me how to get to the bank?

Could you please repeat that?

Would you please tell me how to get to the library?

Say it. Then listen.

Could you please tell me how to get to the park?

Could you please say that again?

Would you please tell me how to get to the zoo?

How do you get to different places in your community? Do you walk? Do you drive? Do you take a bus, train, or subway? Is it easy or difficult to get to these places? Write about it in your journal.

GRAMMAR FOCUS

IMPERATIVES

Walk up Main Street.	**Turn right.**	**Take** the Main Street bus.
Walk down Main Street.	**Turn left.**	**Get off** at First Avenue.
Walk along Central Avenue.		**Drive along** Second Avenue.

Choose the correct word.

1. Turn (along left).
2. (Take Walk) the River Street bus.
3. Get (up off) at Central Avenue.
4. Walk (up right) Third Avenue.
5. (Drive Turn) along Park Street.
6. (Walk Get) off the bus at Fourth Avenue.

Complete these directions with the following words.

across	at	corner	on	Take	turn	Walk
and	blocks	get	see	to	two	

It's easy to get to the hospital from here. Walk up this street _____[1] the corner and _____[2] right. _____[3] three _____[4] and you'll _____[5] a bus stop at the _____[6] of Park Street _____[7] Tenth Avenue. _____[8] the Park Street bus and _____[9] off _____[10] University Road. Walk _____[11] blocks and you'll see the hospital _____[12] the right, _____[13] from the bus station.

1 CONVERSATION Asking For & Giving Schedule Information

CLINIC	
Mon–Fri	8:00 – 7:00
Sat	8:00 – 5:00
Sun	Closed

LIBRARY HOURS	
M, W, F	9:00 AM – 6:30 PM
T, TH	9:00 AM – 9:00 PM
SAT, SUN	10:00 AM – 5:00 PM

POST OFFICE	
M–F	8:00 – 4:00
Sat	8:00 – 1:00
Sun	Closed

Practice the conversations with a classmate.

A. What time does the clinic open on Tuesday?
B. It opens at eight o'clock.

A. What time does the library close on Friday?
B. It closes at six thirty.

A. How many hours is the post office open on Saturday?
B. It's open for five hours.

Now walk around the classroom and practice new conversations with other students. Use the information in the signs above.

A. What time does the ______ open on ______?
B. It opens at ______.

A. What time does the ______ close on ______?
B. It closes at ______.

A. How many hours is the ______ open on ______?
B. It's open for ______ hours.

2 MAILBOX PICKUP TIMES Using Postal Services

Look at the schedule and answer the questions.

How many times do they pick up the mail on weekday mornings? on weekday afternoons? on the weekend?

What time do they pick up the mail on Tuesday morning? on Friday afternoon? on Saturday?

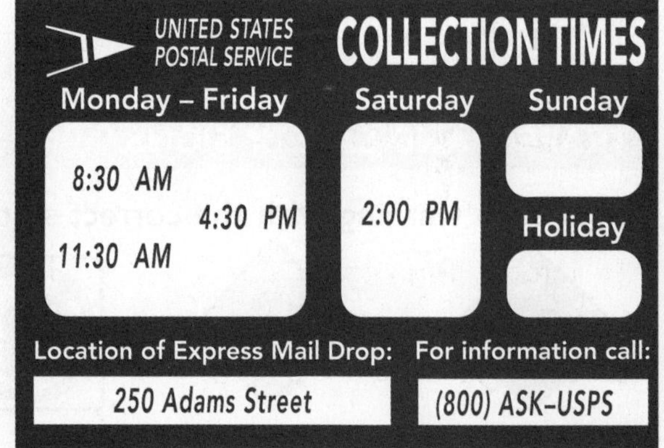

UNITED STATES POSTAL SERVICE
COLLECTION TIMES
Monday – Friday
8:30 AM
4:30 PM
11:30 AM
Saturday
2:00 PM
Sunday
Holiday
Location of Express Mail Drop:
250 Adams Street
For information call:
(800) ASK-USPS

3 COMMUNITY CONNECTIONS Schedules in the Community

Find three schedule signs in your community. Draw the signs, bring them to class, and share with other students. Ask students questions about the schedule information on your signs.

THINK & SHARE Think about schedules of different places in your community. When are these places open? Are the schedules good or bad? Why? What can you do to change a schedule? Discuss with your classmates.

A BUS SCHEDULE

Look at the bus schedule and answer the questions. Circle the answers on the schedule.

High Street	State Street	Kellogg Road	Congress Street	Western Avenue
6:33 AM	6:41 AM	6:54 AM	7:01 AM	7:14 AM
7:48 AM	7:58 AM	8:12 AM	8:24 AM	8:37 AM
8:00 AM	8:10 AM	8:24 AM	8:36 AM	8:49 AM
9:10 AM	9:20 AM	9:33 AM	9:43 AM	9:54 AM
9:50 AM	10:00 AM	——	10:21 AM	10:32 AM
10:30 AM	10:40 AM	——	11:01 AM	11:12 AM
11:00 AM	11:10 AM	11:23 AM	11:33 AM	11:45 AM
11:55 AM	12:05 PM	12:18 PM	12:28 PM	12:39 PM

1. What time does the first bus arrive at Congress Street?
2. When does the 8:00 AM bus get to Kellogg Road?
3. What time does the 10:30 AM bus get to Western Avenue?
4. What time does the 9:50 AM bus arrive at State Street?
5. When does the last morning bus leave from High Street?
6. When does the 7:48 AM bus arrive at Western Avenue?

Choose the correct answers.

7. How long does it take to get from High Street to Kellogg Road at 11:00 AM?
   A. 18 minutes C. 24 minutes
   B. 23 minutes D. 33 minutes

8. You're at the Congress Street bus stop. It's a quarter to nine. When is the next bus?
   A. 8:36 AM C. 9:33 AM
   B. 8:49 AM D. 9:43 AM

9. You're at the State Street bus stop. It's 10:10 AM. How long do you have to wait for a bus?
   A. ten minutes C. half an hour
   B. twenty minutes D. an hour

10. You're meeting someone at the Western Avenue bus stop at 12 noon. When should you leave High Street?
    A. 10:30 AM C. 11:45 AM
    B. 11:00 AM D. 11:55 AM

TRAFFIC AND SAFETY SIGNS

Match each warning with the correct sign.

A

B

C

D

E

F

____ 1. You can't make a left turn here.

____ 2. Slow down. There's a school nearby. Watch for children crossing the road.

____ 3. Traffic from another lane will enter the road.

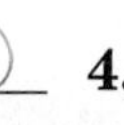
____ 4. Slow down. There's a crosswalk ahead. Watch for pedestrians crossing the road.

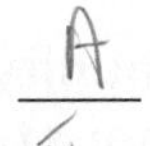
____ 5. Be careful! The road ahead is slippery.

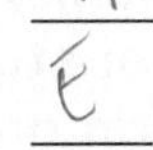
____ 6. The road ahead is closed. Take this road instead.

COMMUNITY CONNECTIONS

Find different traffic signs in your community and draw them. Write down all the words and symbols on the signs. Bring your signs to class, and compare signs with other students.

Safe Driving

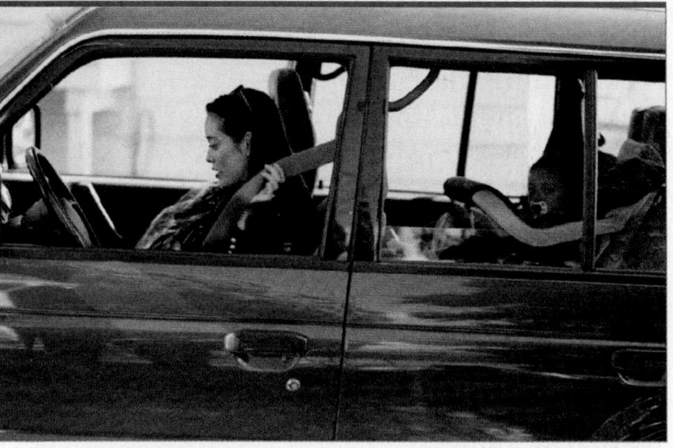

More than 3.5 million people get hurt in car accidents in the United States each year. Here are some things you can do so that you and your passengers are safe.

Always wear a seat belt. Also, make sure that all the passengers in your car wear their seat belts. Children under the age of five should ride in child safety seats that you attach to the back seat of the car. The center back seat is the safest.

Many accidents happen when cars are in bad condition. Take good care of your car. Check the brakes every week to be sure that you can stop the car when you need to. Keep the windshield clean so you can see the road ahead. Be sure the windshield wipers work in the rain.

Be a careful driver. Pay attention to traffic signs, road conditions, and other drivers. Look before you make a turn or change lanes on the highway. Don't "tailgate"—don't stay too close to the car in front of you. The driver might stop without warning. Be especially careful when the weather is bad. Slow down and use your headlights in the rain, snow, and fog. Pay attention to the speed limit. When the speed limit is sixty miles an hour, that's the fastest you should drive. On the other hand, don't be a slow driver. Slow drivers can cause accidents.

You can't pay attention to the road when you're tired or busy doing too many things. Don't eat, drink, or talk on your cell phone while you're driving. Don't take any medicine that can make you sleepy before you drive. The label on such medicine usually has the warning "May cause drowsiness." Remember, other drivers are not always as careful as you are. Be prepared for their mistakes. If you are in an accident, the police will ask to see your papers. Always have your license, car registration, and insurance card with you to show to the police.

1. The best place for a child safety seat is __C__.
A. in the front seat
B. in the back seat next to the door
C. in the center back seat
D. next to the driver

2. According to this article, drivers should __A__.
A. use headlights when it's foggy
B. always drive sixty miles per hour
C. ride in safety seats
D. make mistakes

3. According to this article, drivers should NOT __D__.
A. be prepared for other drivers' mistakes
B. look before changing lanes
C. use their windshield wipers in the rain
D. use a cell phone while they're driving

4. A driver who *tailgates* __B__.
A. is a slow driver
B. drives too close to the car ahead
C. stops without warning
D. is a careful driver

5. We can infer that *the windshield* in paragraph 3 __D__.
A. stops the car
B. cleans the car
C. is in the back of the car
D. is in the front of the car

6. *May cause drowsiness* (drausines) means the medicine __C__.
A. is old
B. is bad for you
C. might make you tired
D. might make you nervous

ASSESSMENT • Check-up test • Self-evaluation checklists

Choose the correct answer.

1. I go to the ___ on Main Street to wash my shirts.
   A. shopping mall
   B. department store
   C. hardware store
   D. laundromat

2. They bake wonderful pies and cakes at the ___ down the street.
   A. bank
   B. bakery
   C. barber shop
   D. flower shop

3. I got off the bus at the wrong ___.
   A. stop
   B. map
   C. bus
   D. directions

4. We don't want to be late for the plane. What's the fastest way to get to the ___?
   A. train station
   B. airport
   C. bus station
   D. gas station

5. Can you ___ a good department store in a convenient location?
   A. tell me how
   B. directions
   C. how to get there
   D. recommend

6. What ___ does the clinic close on Monday?
   A. hours
   B. schedule
   C. time
   D. schedule sign

7. When you drive, you should always ___.
   A. ride in a child safety seat
   B. wear a seat belt
   C. tailgate
   D. be a slow driver

8. When you drive, don't ___.
   A. drive and talk on your cell phone
   B. use your headlights in the fog
   C. look before you change lanes
   D. pay attention to the speed limit

Look at the bus schedule. Choose the correct answer.

9. You're at the Lake Street bus stop. It's half past seven. The next bus is at ___.
   A. 6:15 AM
   B. 7:10 AM
   C. 7:55 AM
   D. 8:30 AM

10. You're at the Main Street bus stop. It's a quarter after eight. You have to wait ___ for the next bus.
   A. 6 minutes
   B. 21 minutes
   C. 8:21
   D. 8:51

Lake St.	First Ave.	Main St.	River Rd.
6:15 AM	6:24 AM	6:36 AM	6:42 AM
7:10 AM	7:21 AM	7:34 AM	7:42 AM
7:55 AM	8:07 AM	8:21 AM	8:29 AM
8:30 AM	8:40 AM	8:51AM	8:58 AM

SKILLS CHECK

Words:

- ☐ airport
- ☐ bakery
- ☐ bank
- ☐ barber shop
- ☐ baseball stadium
- ☐ book store
- ☐ bus station
- ☐ cafeteria
- ☐ church
- ☐ clinic
- ☐ concert hall
- ☐ courthouse
- ☐ department store
- ☐ drug store
- ☐ fire station
- ☐ flower shop
- ☐ gas station
- ☐ hardware store
- ☐ high school
- ☐ hospital
- ☐ hotel
- ☐ ice cream shop
- ☐ laundromat
- ☐ library
- ☐ motel
- ☐ museum
- ☐ park
- ☐ parking garage
- ☐ parking lot
- ☐ pet shop
- ☐ playground
- ☐ police station
- ☐ post office
- ☐ restaurant
- ☐ shoe store
- ☐ shopping mall
- ☐ supermarket
- ☐ toy store
- ☐ train station
- ☐ university
- ☐ zoo
- ☐ back seat
- ☐ brakes
- ☐ child safety seat
- ☐ headlights
- ☐ passenger
- ☐ road conditions
- ☐ seat belt
- ☐ speed limit
- ☐ tailgate
- ☐ traffic sign
- ☐ windshield
- ☐ windshield wipers

I can ask & answer:

- ☐ Can you tell me/Could you please tell me/Would you please tell me how to get *there*?
- ☐ What's the quickest/easiest way to get to the *bank*?
- ☐ What time does the *clinic* open/close on *Tuesday*?

I can read:

- ☐ schedule information on signs
- ☐ a bus schedule
- ☐ traffic & safety signs

I can:

- ☐ draw a map and write directions

I can write about:

- ☐ ways I get to places in my community

8

Adverbs
Comparative of Adverbs
Agent Nouns
If-Clauses

- Describing People's Actions
- Describing Plans and Intentions
- Consequences of Actions
- Job Interview
- Stating Skills and Work Experience
- Asking for Permission at Work
- Help Wanted Ads
- Reading a Paycheck and Pay Stub
- Employee Accident Report

Vocabulary Preview

1. actor
2. dancer
3. driver
4. painter
5. player
6. runner
7. singer
8. skier
9. teacher
10. translator
11. worker

He Drives Very Carelessly

slow – slowly
careless – carelessly

careful – carefully
graceful – gracefully

fast – fast
hard – hard

good – well

A. I think he's **a careless driver**.

B. I agree. He **drives VERY carelessly**.

1. *a careful worker*

2. *a slow chess player*

3. *a graceful dancer*

4. *good actors*

5. *a careless skier*

6. *a fast runner*

7. *a beautiful singer*

8. *bad painters*

9. *a good teacher*

10. *a hard worker*

11. *an accurate translator*

12. *dishonest card players*

You Should Work Faster

fast – faster quickly – quicker* loud(ly) – louder* slowly – slower*	carefully – more carefully gracefully – more gracefully accurately – more accurately	well – better

A. Am I working **fast** enough?

B. Actually, you should work **faster**.

A. Am I painting **carefully** enough?

B. Actually, you should paint **more carefully**.

1. Am I typing quickly enough?

2. Am I dancing gracefully enough?

3. Am I speaking loud enough?

4. Am I driving slowly enough?

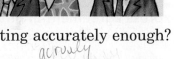

5. Am I translating accurately enough?

6. Am I playing well enough?

* *quicker* or *more quickly* *louder* or *more loudly* *slower* or *more slowly*

He Should Try to Speak Slower

loud(ly) – louder*	slowly – slower*
neatly – neater*	softly – softer*
quickly – quicker*	

carefully – more carefully
politely – more politely

early – earlier
late – later

well – better

A. Bob speaks VERY **quickly**.

B. You're right. He should try to speak **slower**.

1. Timothy types very slowly.

2. Carol skates very carelessly.

3. Howard speaks very softly.

4. Linda goes to bed very late.

5. Jimmy gets up very early.

6. They dress very sloppily.

7. Brenda plays her radio very loudly.

8. Richard speaks to his parents very impolitely.

9. Our next-door neighbor drives very badly.

How to Say It!

Expressing Agreement

You're right.
That's right.
That's true.
I know.
I agree.
I agree with you.

Practice the conversations on this page again. Express agreement in different ways.

* *louder* or *more loudly* *neater* or *more neatly* *quicker* or *more quickly* *slower* or *more slowly* *softer* or *more softly*

READING

TRYING HARDER

Michael's boss talked with him today. In general, she doesn't think Michael is doing very well on the job. He has to do better. According to Michael's boss, he types too slowly. He should type faster. In addition, he files too carelessly. He should file more carefully. Furthermore, he speaks on the telephone too quickly. He should speak slower. Michael wants to do well on the job, and he knows now that he has to try a little harder.

Stella's director talked with her today. In general, he doesn't think Stella is doing very well in his play. She has to do better. According to Stella's director, she speaks too softly. She should speak louder. In addition, she walks too slowly. She should walk faster. Furthermore, she dances too awkwardly. She should dance more gracefully. Stella wants to do well in the play, and she knows now that she has to try a little harder.

Billy's teacher talked with him today. In general, she doesn't think Billy is doing very well in school. He has to do better. According to Billy's teacher, he arrives at school too late. He should arrive earlier. In addition, he dresses too sloppily. He should dress more neatly. Furthermore, he speaks too impolitely. He should speak more politely. Billy wants to do well in school, and he knows now that he has to try a little harder.

READING *CHECK-UP*

Q & A

Michael is talking with his boss. Stella is talking with her director. Billy is talking with his teacher. Using this model, create dialogs based on the story.

A. Do I *type fast* enough?
B. No. You *type* too *slowly*.
A. Oh. I'll try to *type faster* in the future.

WHAT'S THE OPPOSITE?

1. quickly (*slowly*)
2. carefully
3. loudly
4. politely
5. badly
6. sloppily
7. awkwardly
8. earlier
9. faster

If

If ______________ will ______________

A. What are they going to name their new baby?

B. If they have a boy, they'll name him John.
If they have a girl, they'll name her Jane.

1. A. How are you going to get to school tomorrow?

B. If it rains, I'll ___take the bus___.
If it's sunny, I'll ___walk___.

2. A. What's Roger going to do this Saturday afternoon?

B. If the weather is good, he'll ___go to the beach___.
If the weather is bad, he'll ___go to the movies___.

3. A. What's Rosa going to have for dinner tonight?

B. If she's very hungry, ___she'll go___.
If she isn't very hungry, ___she'll have a___.

4. A. What's Ken going to do tomorrow?

B. If he feels better, ___he'll go to work___.
If he doesn't feel better, ___he'll go to the D___.

How About You?

What are you going to do tonight if you have a lot of homework?	What are you going to wear tomorrow if it's warm and sunny?	What are you going to do this weekend if the weather is nice?
What are you going to do tonight if you DON'T have a lot of homework?	What are you going to wear tomorrow if it's cool and raining?	What are you going to do this weekend if the weather is bad?

If You Drive Too Fast, You Might Have an Accident

If ______________ might ______________

A. You know . . . you shouldn't drive so fast.

B. Oh?

A. Yes. If you drive too fast, you might have an accident.

B. Hmm. You're probably right.

1. *eat so quickly*
get a stomachache

2. *sing so loudly*
get a sore throat

3. *work so slowly*
lose your job

4. *go to bed so late*
be tired in the morning

5. *listen to loud music*
hurt your ears

6. *watch scary movies*
have nightmares

7. *do your homework so carelessly*
make mistakes

8. *sit at your computer so long*
get a backache

9.

READING

GOOD DECISIONS

Ronald wants to stay up late to watch a movie tonight, but he knows he shouldn't. If he stays up late to watch a movie, he won't get to bed until after midnight. If he doesn't get to bed until after midnight, he'll be very tired in the morning. If he's very tired in the morning, he might oversleep. If he oversleeps, he'll be late for work. If he's late for work, his boss might get angry and fire him. So, even though Ronald wants to stay up late to watch a movie tonight, he isn't going to. Good decision, Ronald!

Barbara wants to buy a new car, but she knows she shouldn't. If she buys a new car, she'll have to take a lot of money out of her bank account. If she has to take a lot of money out of her bank account, she won't have much left. If she doesn't have much left, she won't have enough money to pay the rent. If she doesn't have enough money to pay the rent, her landlord might evict her from her apartment. So, even though Barbara wants to buy a new car, she isn't going to. Good decision, Barbara!

✓ READING *CHECK-UP*

WHICH WORD IS CORRECT?

1. If Ronald (doesn't won't) go to bed early, he'll be (angry tired) in the morning.
2. If (he's he'll) late for work, his boss might (watch fire) him.
3. If Barbara (buy buys) a new car, she (won't doesn't) have much money left.
4. If she (should doesn't) pay her rent, her landlord might (account evict) her.
5. Even though Ronald and Barbara (won't want) to do these things, they (are aren't) going to.

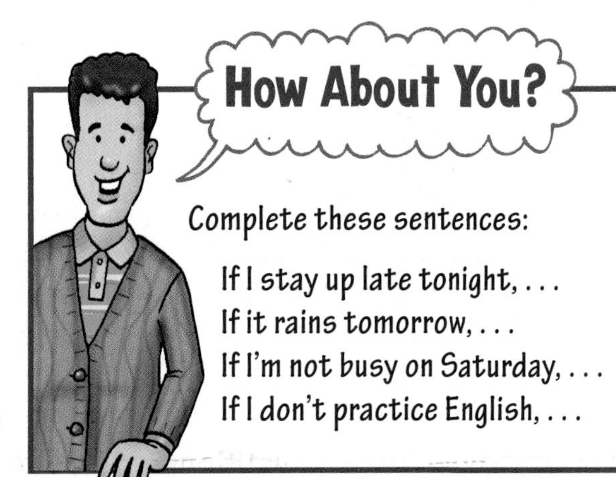

Complete these sentences:

If I stay up late tonight, . . .
If it rains tomorrow, . . .
If I'm not busy on Saturday, . . .
If I don't practice English, . . .

LISTENING

Listen and choose the best answer to complete the sentence.

1. (a.) my teacher will be happy.
   (b.) my teacher won't be happy.
2. (a.) she won't go back to school.
   b. she'll go back to school.
3. a. you'll get a sore throat.
   (b.) you might get a backache.
4. a. I'll be early in the future.
   (b.) I'll be tired in the morning.
5. a. people will hear you.
   (b.) people won't hear you.
6. (a.) your boss might fire you.
   b. your landlord might evict you.

ON YOUR OWN *Superstitions*

Many people believe that you'll have GOOD luck . . .

if you find a four-leaf clover.
if you find a horseshoe.
if you give a new pair of shoes to a poor person.

Many people believe that you'll have BAD luck . . .

if a black cat walks in front of you.
if you walk under a ladder.
if you open an umbrella in your home.
if you put your shoes on a table.

Here are some other superstitions:

If your right eye itches, you'll laugh soon.
If your left eye itches, you'll cry soon.

If your right ear itches, somebody is saying good things about you.
If your left ear itches, somebody is saying bad things about you.

If a knife falls, a man will visit soon.
If a fork falls, a woman will visit soon.
If a spoon falls, a baby will visit soon.

If you break a mirror, you'll have bad luck for seven years.

Do you know any superstitions? Share them with other students in your class.

PRONUNCIATION Contrastive Stress

Listen. Then say it.

If it ráins, I'll go to the móvies.
If it's súnny, I'll go to the béach.

If they have a bóy, they'll name him Jóhn.
If they have a gírl, they'll name her Jáne.

If she's tíred, she'll go to bed éarly.
If she ísn't tired, she'll go to bed láte.

Say it. Then listen.

If it's hót, I'll wear a tée shirt.
If it's cóld, I'll wear a swéater.

If we work quíckly, we'll finish éarly.
If we work slówly, we'll finish láte.

If he speaks lóudly, people will héar him.
If he dóesn't speak loudly, people wón't hear him.

**Think about something you want to do.
If you do it, what will happen?
Write about it in your journal.**

GRAMMAR FOCUS

ADVERBS

He works	slowly. carefully. sloppily. fast. hard. well.

COMPARATIVE OF ADVERBS

He should try to work	quicker. more quickly.
	more carefully. more accurately.
	faster. harder. better.

AGENT NOUNS

actor	singer
dancer	skier
driver	teacher
painter	translator
player	worker
runner	

Choose the correct word.

1. Roger is a (slow slowly) driver. He drives very (slow slowly).
2. Angela is a (careful carefully) worker. She works very (careful carefully).
3. Mrs. Chang teaches very (good well). She's a (good well) teacher.
4. Jim always arrives at the office too (late later). He should arrive (later earlier).

IF-CLAUSES

If	I we you they	feel	better,	I'll we'll you'll they'll	go to work.
	he she it	feels		he'll she'll it'll	

If	I'm we're you're they're	tired,	I'll we'll you'll they'll	go to sleep early.
	he's she's it's		he'll she'll it'll	

Choose the correct word.

5. If (I I'm) hungry, (I'm I'll) have a big dinner.
6. If (she she'll) goes to bed late, (she she'll) be tired tomorrow.
7. If (you'll you) eat too fast, (you'll you) get sick.
8. If it (rains will rain) tomorrow, (we'll we) go to the movies.

1 CONVERSATION Describing Job Interest, Skills, & Work History

Look at the job application forms. Practice conversations with your classmates.

A. What kind of job are you looking for?
B. I'm looking for a job as a/an ________.
A. Tell me about your skills.
B. I can ________, and I can ________.
A. Where do you work now?
B. I work at ________.
A. And where did you work before that?
B. I worked at ________.

1. 

Position Desired: waitress
Skills: take orders, serve customers
EMPLOYMENT
Current: Jake's Restaurant
Previous: the Main Street Diner

2. 

Position Desired: auto mechanic
Skills: fix cars, tune up engines
EMPLOYMENT
Current: Ahmed's Car Repair
Previous: County Line Auto Shop

3. 

Position Desired: electrician
Skills: install light fixtures, wire a house
EMPLOYMENT
Current: Ajax Electrical Services
Previous: City Light & Power Company

4. 

Position Desired: medical technician
Skills: take blood samples, do lab tests
EMPLOYMENT
Current: Memorial Hospital
Previous: Bay Shore Laboratory

2 TEAMWORK Preparing For a Job Interview

Work with a classmate. Fill out the form with your information. Then practice job interview conversations.

Position Desired: ________
Skills: ________
EMPLOYMENT
Current: ________
Previous: ________

3 CONVERSATION Requesting a Schedule Change

Practice this conversation between an employee and a supervisor at work.

A. Excuse me, Mr. Harris.
B. Yes?
A. Could I possibly leave early today? The reason is I have to take my mother to the doctor.
B. I understand. Yes. That'll be okay.
A. Thank you very much.

Now practice conversations with different classmates. Use your last names in the conversations.

1. take the day off next Monday
I have to go to court.

2. take a break
I don't feel well. I need to sit down.

3. leave now
The school nurse called. My daughter is sick.

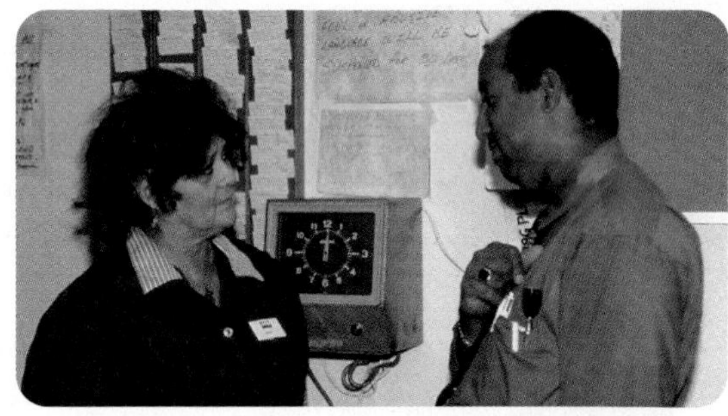

4. come in an hour late on Friday morning
I have a parent-teacher conference at my son's school.

4 TEAMWORK Critical Thinking

Work with a classmate. What are some good reasons to ask for a change in schedule or time off from work? What are some bad reasons? Make two lists. Then discuss with your classmates.

Good Reasons	Bad Reasons
______________	______________
______________	______________
______________	______________

Look at the help wanted ads and answer the questions.

CASHIER
Donut shop needs PT cashier. 2 weekday nights, 7 P.M.–11 P.M. & 2 weekend days, 8 A.M.– 4 P.M. $9+/hr. Apply in person at Mr. Donut, 850 Willow Avenue.

CHEF
Fine restaurant needs FT chef. Prepare & cook appetizers, soups, vegetables, desserts. Supervise 5 employees. 2 yrs. exper. req. Excel. salary & benefits. Send 2 copies of resume to Carrington Restaurant, 53 Ames St., Bridgeport, CA.

CUSTODIAN
FT. $8.00/hr. M–F, 10 P.M.–5 A.M. Clean offices, vacuum carpets, operate floor machines, clean restrooms. 1 yr. exper. pref. Call 760-467-9000. Ask for Gordon.

DRIVERS WANTED
Looking for drivers to deliver the Bridgeport Herald. PT, 7 days/wk early morning. $950–$1,050/mo. Must have reliable car, valid CA driver's license, & clean driving record. Call Mark. 760-983-1945.

RECEPTIONIST NEEDED
PT, $7.50–$8/hr. Answer phones, file, get customer information. Must have high school diploma. Good English language and telephone skills req. Spanish speaker pref. Call Rita at 760-846-3700.

RESTAURANT HELP
New restaurant now hiring FT dishwashers, PT waitpersons. Exper. pref., but not req. Will train. Apply in person. Harbor Restaurant, 350 Ocean Drive. No phone calls, please.

SALESPEOPLE
FT & PT positions starting at $9/hr. Work days or eves. No exper. req. Call 760-965-3400 ext. 47 or apply in person at P. T. Jones and Company, 457 Forest Ave.

SECRETARY
FT position in busy doctors' office. Excel. computer skills & 2+ yrs. exper. req. Excel. salary & medical benefits. Send resume to Mt. Pleasant Medical Associates, 1240 Main St., Bridgeport, CA.

1. The Harbor Restaurant needs ____.
A. part-time dishwashers
B. a full-time chef
C. part-time waiters and waitresses
D. a part-time cashier

2. The custodian does NOT have to ____.
A. clean offices
B. vacuum carpets
C. operate floor machines
D. have a clean driving record

3. The drivers work ____.
A. forty hours a week
B. seven mornings a week
C. eight hours a day
D. evenings

4. The cashier at Mr. Donut has to work ____.
A. Sunday morning
B. Wednesday evening
C. Saturday night
D. Monday afternoon

5. Apply in person for the job as ____.
A. a driver
B. a secretary
C. a receptionist
D. a dishwasher

6. Send two copies of your resume to ____.
A. P.T. Jones and Company
B. Mt. Pleasant Medical Associates
C. Carrington Restaurant
D. Harbor Restaurant

7. Experience is required for the job ____.
A. at Harbor Restaurant
B. at P.T. Jones and Company
C. as a custodian
D. at Mt. Pleasant Medical Associates

8. The receptionist does NOT have to ____.
A. have a high school diploma
B. speak Spanish
C. have good English language skills
D. have good telephone skills

TEAMWORK Cut out some help wanted ads from the newspaper and bring them to class. Work with a classmate. Compare ads for different jobs. What information is in the ads? How should people apply for the jobs?

Look at the paycheck and pay stub and answer the questions.

FOSTER COMPANY LAM M. EMP. NO. 46803

PAY PERIOD 06/30/10 – 07/06/10

PAY DATE: 07/11/10

EARNINGS	RATE	HOURS	THIS PERIOD	YEAR TO DATE
REGULAR	11.00	32	352.00	11,440.00
OVERTIME	16.50	2	33.00	319.00
HOLIDAY	22.00	8	176.00	528.00
GROSS PAY			561.00	12,287.00

	THIS PERIOD	YEAR TO DATE		
FED TAX	37.84	975.92	TAXES	92.94
FICA/MED	36.18	933.22	DEDUCTIONS	42.25
STATE TAX	18.92	487.96		
HEALTH	42.25	1,140.75		
			NET PAY	425.81

GROSS PAY 561.00

FOSTER COMPANY

Check No. 2689412

Date Issued 07/11/10

Pay to MEI LAM

FOUR HUNDRED TWENTY-FIVE DOLLARS AND EIGHTY-ONE CENTS ***$425.81

Rosemary Martinez

1. Mei's regular pay is ____.
   A. $8.00 an hour C. $16.50 an hour
   B. $11.00 an hour D. $32.00 an hour

2. Mei earned ____ when she worked on the July 4th holiday during this pay period.
   A. $11.00 an hour C. $176.00
   B. $16.50 an hour D. $528.00

3. Mei worked ____ this pay period.
   A. 32 hours C. 40 hours
   B. 34 hours D. 42 hours

4. A pay period at this company is ____.
   A. a week C. a month
   B. a day D. a year

5. Mei earned ____ before taxes and other deductions.
   A. $92.94 C. $425.81
   B. $352.00 D. $561.00

6. The deduction for state taxes was ____.
   A. $18.92 C. $37.84
   B. $36.18 D. $42.25

7. Mei paid $1,140.75 this year for ____.
   A. federal taxes C. state taxes
   B. health insurance D. overtime

8. Mei earned ____ from 1/1/10 to 7/6/10.
   A. $975.92 C. $11,440.00
   B. $1,140.75 D. $12,287.00

THINK & SHARE What taxes and deductions do you see on the pay stub in this lesson? What do these taxes and deductions pay for? Discuss as a class.

Look at the employee accident report and answer the questions.

HILLER HOTEL EMPLOYEE ACCIDENT REPORT

PLEASE COMPLETE AND SUBMIT TO THE PERSONNEL DEPARTMENT.

Name of injured employee: Orlando Cortina		SS# 289-43-6708	SEX: ✓ M F
Home address of employee: 89 Carleton Road, Cloverleaf, TX 77015			Date of Birth: 5/22/80
Job Title: Custodian	Department: Maintenance		Date of Report: 10/01/12
Where did accident occur? Laundry room, basement			Date of Accident: 9/23/12
Time of Accident: 11:30 (A.M.) P.M.	Names of Witnesses: Paula Sanders, Jane Ling		
Nature of injury and part(s) of body injured: I broke my left arm.			
How did the employee get injured? I went to the laundry room to fix a broken shelf. I was on a ladder. The ladder moved, and I fell off.			
What safety equipment, if any, did employee use? None			
What factors contributed to the accident? The floor was wet and slippery. There wasn't enough light.			
Did employee lose time from work? Yes	How much time? One week		
Physician's name: Dr. Rafael Garcia	Address: 78 Forest Avenue, Cloverleaf, TX 77015		
Immediate Supervisor signature: Alice Winter			Date signed: 10/01/12
Department Head signature: Carlo Marconi			Date signed: 10/01/12
Employee signature: Orlando Cortina			Date signed: 10/01/12

1. What is Orlando Cortina's job?
   A. He's a laundry worker.
   B. He's a physician.
   C. He's a supervisor.
   (D.) He's a custodian.

2. When was the accident?
   A. On May twenty-second.
   (B.) On September twenty-third.
   C. On October first.
   D. At 11:30 at night.

3. Who saw the accident?
   A. Alice Winter.
   B. Carlo Marconi.
   C. Dr. Rafael Garcia.
   (D.) Paula Sanders and Jane Ling.

4. Why did Orlando go to the laundry room?
   (A.) To fix a shelf.
   B. To do the laundry.
   C. To move a ladder.
   D. To fix a ladder.

5. Who should Orlando give this report to?
   A. The maintenance department.
   (B.) The personnel department.
   C. His physician.
   D. His supervisor.

6. What DIDN'T Orlando do?
   A. He didn't break his left arm.
   B. He didn't fall off a ladder.
   (C.) He didn't use safety equipment.
   D. He didn't sign the accident report.

THINK & SHARE What kinds of accidents and injuries can happen at different workplaces you know? How can employers and employees prevent these accidents and injuries? Share ideas as a class.

ASSESSMENT • Check-up test • Self-evaluation checklists

Choose the correct answer.

1. Timothy isn't a good dancer. He dances ____.
   A. awkwardly
   B. beautifully
   C. gracefully
   D. very well

2. If you want to finish this report today, you'll have to work more ____.
   A. slowly
   B. quickly
   C. carelessly
   D. sloppily

3. I'm sorry. I can't hear you. You aren't speaking ____ enough.
   A. softly
   B. fast
   C. quickly
   D. loud

4. Barry's boss likes him because he always ____.
   A. arrives late for work
   B. speaks impolitely
   C. dresses sloppily
   D. gets to work early

5. I can fix cars and tune up engines. I have good ____ to be a mechanic.
   A. work
   B. job
   C. skills
   D. employment

6. ____, Ms. Carson. Could I possibly leave work early today?
   A. Excuse me
   B. The reason is
   C. That'll be okay
   D. Thank you very much

7. Marcela earned ____ this pay period.
   A. 40 hours
   B. $127.50
   C. federal taxes
   D. health insurance

8. Anna had an accident at work. She completed and submitted ____.
   A. her supervisor
   B. three witnesses
   C. her physician
   D. an accident report

Look at the help wanted ads. Choose the correct answer.

9. The salesperson doesn't have to ____.
   A. work in the morning
   B. apply in person
   C. work on Sunday
   D. go to Washington Street

10. Experience is required for the ____.
   A. full-time job
   B. job at the Maxwell Company
   C. job as a cashier
   D. job as a salesperson

CASHIER
Drug store needs PT cashier 3 weekday afts. 1 P.M.–5:30 P.M. & 2 weekend mornings 8:00 A.M.–11:30 A.M. $11/hr. Exper. pref., but not req. Call Ms. Lee at 775-220-4574.

CUSTODIAN
PT. $9.00/hr. 4 weekday mornings 8:00 A.M.–11:00 A.M. & 2 weekend afternoons 2:00 P.M.–5:00 P.M. 2 yrs. exper. req. Apply in person at the Maxwell Company, 451 Winter St.

SALESPERSON
FT position starting at $10/hr. 9:30 A.M.–6:00 P.M. M–Sat. No exper. req. Apply in person. Saxony Department Store, 943 Washington St.

SKILLS CHECK ☑

Words:
- ☐ accurate – accurately
- ☐ awkward – awkwardly
- ☐ bad – badly
- ☐ beautiful – beautifully
- ☐ careful – carefully
- ☐ careless – carelessly
- ☐ dishonest – dishonestly
- ☐ fast – fast
- ☐ good – well
- ☐ graceful – gracefully
- ☐ hard – hard
- ☐ impolite – impolitely
- ☐ loud – loud(ly)
- ☐ neat – neat(ly)
- ☐ polite – politely
- ☐ quick – quickly
- ☐ sloppy – sloppily
- ☐ slow – slowly
- ☐ soft – softly

I can ask & answer:
- ☐ Am I *working fast* enough? Actually, you should *work faster.*
- ☐ What are you going to do *tomorrow*? If ____, I'll ____.
- ☐ What kind of job are you looking for?
- ☐ Tell me about your skills.
- ☐ Where do you work now?
- ☐ And where did you work before that?
- ☐ Could I possibly *leave early today*? The reason is ____.

I can express agreement:
- ☐ You're right./That's right./ That's true./I know./I agree./ I agree with you.

I can write about:
- ☐ consequences of my actions

I can interpret:
- ☐ help wanted ads
- ☐ a paycheck and pay stub
- ☐ an employee accident report

SIDE by SIDE Gazette

Volume 2 Number 3

You're Hired!

Ten tips for a successful job interview!

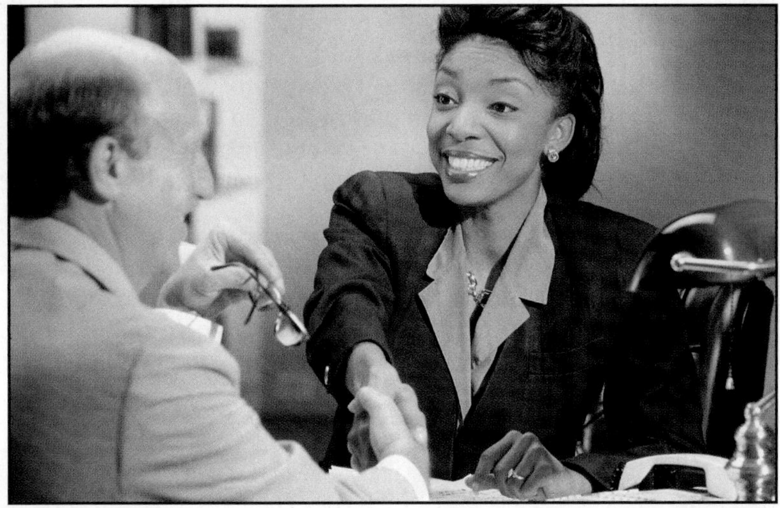

We asked personnel officers at companies in New York, Los Angeles, Toronto, Miami, Chicago, and Vancouver: What should job applicants do to have a successful job interview? Here is their advice:

1. Dress neatly. Don't dress sloppily. Comb your hair neatly.
2. Arrive promptly. Don't be late for your interview. Try to arrive early.
3. Shake hands firmly. A firm handshake shows that you are a friendly and confident person.
4. Look at the interviewer directly. Make "eye contact." Smile!
5. Listen carefully to the interviewer. Listen to the questions carefully so you can answer accurately.
6. Speak politely. Don't speak too quickly, and don't speak too loudly or softly.
7. Answer questions honestly. Tell the truth.
8. Speak confidently. Describe your skills and experience completely. If you don't have experience, you should talk about how you can learn quickly.
9. Speak enthusiastically. Show that you really want the job!
10. Send a thank-you note promptly. Thank the interviewer for his or her time and express again your interest in the job.

Some of these tips might not be correct in some cultures—for example, a firm handshake or eye contact. Are these tips correct in different cultures you know? What are other tips for job interviews in these cultures?

BUILD YOUR VOCABULARY!

Occupations

I'm a/an ___________ .

■ assembler

■ designer

■ director

■ gardener

■ inspector

■ photographer

■ programmer

■ supervisor

■ welder

■ writer

AROUND THE WORLD

Men and Women at Work

The jobs that men and women have are changing in many countries around the world.

a construction worker in Vietnam

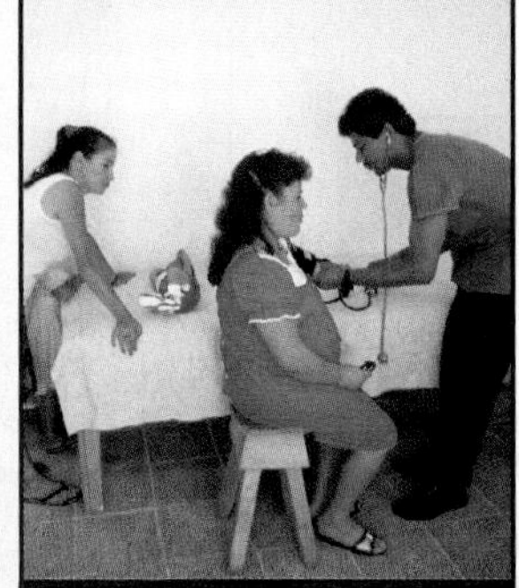

a nurse in Costa Rica

a teacher in Bangladesh

a company president in France

an airline pilot in England

a homemaker in the United States

What jobs do men and women usually have in different countries you know? Is this changing?

Global Exchange

Glen25: In your last message, you asked me to tell you more about myself. So I will. I'm very athletic. I get up early every morning, and I run for an hour. My friends say I'm a fast runner. I'm also a hard worker. I work very hard at school. I'm a good driver. I drive very carefully. I'm not a good dancer. I don't dance very well. I'm not really a very shy person, but everybody tells me I speak softly. And I like to play the piano. I play pretty well, but I want to play better, so I have a piano lesson every week. How about you? Tell me more about yourself.

Send a message to a keypal. Tell a little about yourself. (Remember: Don't give your full name or other personal information when you communicate with people online.)

LISTENING

Attention, All Employees!

d	1 Workplace 1	a.	neatly
c	2 Workplace 2	b.	early
a	3 Workplace 3	c.	quickly
e	4 Workplace 4	d.	carefully
b	5 Workplace 5	e.	loudly

What Are They Saying?

9

Past Continuous Tense
Reflexive Pronouns
While-Clauses

- Describing Ongoing Past Activities
- Reporting a Home Emergency
- Emergency Preparedness
- First-Aid Instructions
- Warning Labels on Household Products
- Safety Procedures: Earthquakes and Hurricanes

Vocabulary Preview

1. bite
2. break into
3. crash into
4. drop
5. faint
6. fall
7. lose
8. spill
9. trip
10. get on
11. get off
12. get out of
13. burn myself
14. cut myself
15. hurt myself

The Blackout

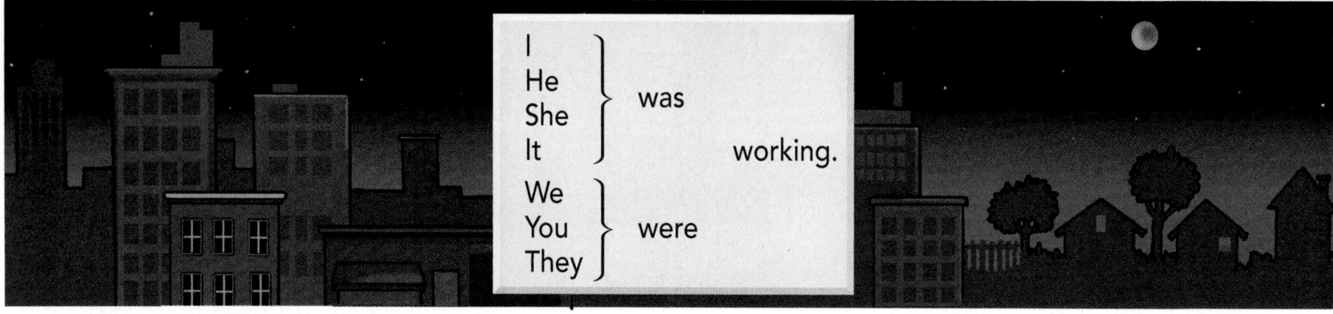

I / He / She / It	was	working.
We / You / They	were	

Last night at 8:00 there was a blackout in Centerville. The lights went out all over town.

A. What was Doris doing last night when the lights went out?

B. She was taking a bath.

A. What were Mr. and Mrs. Green doing last night when the lights went out?

B. They were riding in the elevator.

1. *David*

2. *Mr. and Mrs. Park*

3. *Helen*

4. *you and your brother*

5. *you*

6. *Larry*

7. *Alice*

8. *your parents*

9. *your cousin Sam*

What were YOU doing last night at 8:00?

I Saw You Yesterday, but You Didn't See Me

A. I saw you yesterday, but you didn't see me.

B. Really? When?

A. At about 2:30. You were **getting out of a taxi on Main Street**.

B. That wasn't me. Yesterday at 2:30 I was **cooking dinner**.

A. Hmm. I guess I made a mistake.

1. *walking into the laundromat*
working at my office

2. *walking out of the library*
taking a history test

3. *getting on a bus*
visiting my grandparents

4. *getting off a merry-go-round*
practicing the piano

5. *jogging through the park*
fixing my bathroom sink

6.

READING

A ROBBERY

There was a robbery at 151 River Street yesterday afternoon. Burglars broke* into every apartment in the building while all the tenants were out.

The man in Apartment 1 wasn't home. He was washing his clothes at the laundromat. The woman in Apartment 2 wasn't home either. She was visiting a friend in the hospital. The people in Apartment 3 were gone. They were having a picnic at the beach. The man in Apartment 4 was out. He was playing tennis in the park. The college students in Apartment 5 were away. They were attending a football game. And the elderly lady in Apartment 6 was out of town. She was visiting her grandchildren in Ohio.

Yesterday certainly was an unfortunate day for the people at 151 River Street. They had no idea that while they were away, burglars broke into every apartment in the building.

* break – broke

READING *CHECK-UP*

Q & A

The tenants at 151 River Street are talking to the police. Using this model, create dialogs based on the story.

A. Which apartment do you live in?
B. Apartment *1*.
A. Were you home at the time of the robbery?
B. No, *I wasn't. I was washing my clothes at the laundromat.*
A. What did the burglars take from your apartment?
B. They took *my VCR*, *my computer*, and some money *I* had in *a drawer in my bedroom.*
A. How much money did they take?
B. About *three hundred dollars.*

He Went to the Movies by Himself

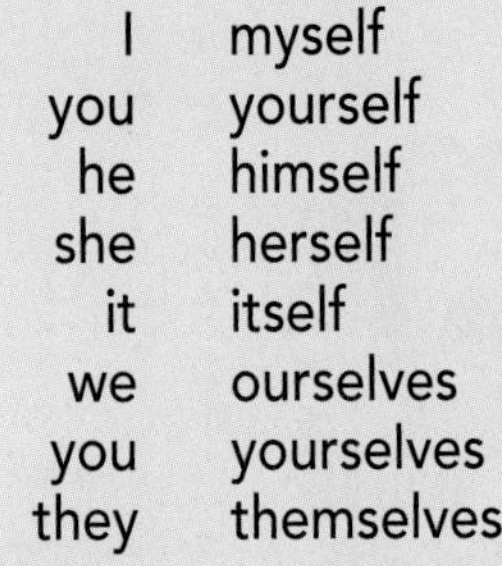

I	myself
you	yourself
he	himself
she	herself
it	itself
we	ourselves
you	yourselves
they	themselves

A. What did **John** do yesterday?

B. He went to the movies.

A. Oh. Who did he go to the movies with?

B. Nobody. He went to the movies **by himself**.

1. *Aunt Ethel*
go to the circus

2. *your parents*
go sailing

3. *you and your wife*
have a picnic

4. *Ann*
drive to the mountains

5. *you*
go bowling

6. *your brother and sister*
play volleyball

7. *Grandma*
take a walk in the park

8. *Uncle Joe*
go fishing

9.

I Had a Bad Day Today

while

A. You look upset.

B. I had a bad day today.

A. Why? What happened?

B. I lost my wallet while I was jogging through the park.

A. I'm sorry to hear that.

A. Harry looks upset.

B. He had a bad day today.

A. Why? What happened?

B. He cut* himself while he was shaving.

A. I'm sorry to hear that.

1. *you*
hurt myself*
fixing my fence

2. *Emma*
dropped her packages
walking out of the supermarket

3. *your parents*
got a flat tire
driving over a bridge

* cut – cut hurt – hurt

4. *Henry*
*tripped and fell**
walking down the stairs

5. *you*
burned myself
cooking on the barbecue

BUS STOP

6. *Wilma*
fainted
waiting for the bus

7. *you and your husband*
somebody stole our car
shopping

8. *you*
a can of paint fell on me
walking under a ladder

9. *the mail carrier*
a dog bit him*
delivering the mail

How to Say It!

Reacting to Bad News

I'm sorry to hear that.
That's too bad!

That's terrible!

That's a shame!

What a shame!

What a pity!

How awful!

Practice the conversations in this lesson again. React to the bad news in different ways.

How About You?

Everybody has a bad day once in a while. Can you remember when something bad happened to you? What happened, and what were you doing when it happened?

* fall – fell bite – bit

FRIDAY THE 13TH

Yesterday was Friday the 13th. Many people believe that Friday the 13th is a very unlucky day. I, myself, didn't think so . . . until yesterday.

Yesterday I burned myself while I was cooking breakfast.

My wife cut herself while she was opening a package.

My son poked himself in the eye while he was putting on his glasses.

Our daughter spilled milk all over herself while she was eating lunch.

Both our children fell and hurt themselves while they were roller-blading.

And we all got wet paint all over ourselves while we were sitting on a bench in the park.

I'm not usually superstitious, but yesterday was a very unlucky day. So, the next time it's Friday the 13th, do yourself a favor! Take care of yourself!

✔ READING *CHECK-UP*

Q & A

The man in the story is talking with a friend. Using this model, create dialogs based on the story.

A. *My wife* had a bad day yesterday.
B. Oh? What happened?
A. *She cut herself* while *she was opening a package.*
B. That's too bad!

WHICH WORD IS CORRECT?

1. He __a__ himself while he was cooking.
   a. burned b. cut
2. His daughter spilled __b__.
   a. paint b. milk
3. His son poked himself in the __a__.
   a. eye b. glasses
4. His children fell and hurt __b__.
   a. ourselves b. themselves
5. We got wet paint all over __a__.
   a. ourselves b. themselves

LISTENING

Listen to the conversations. What happened to these people? Listen and choose the correct answer.

1. a. He cut himself.
   b. He dropped his packages.
2. a. She tripped.
   b. She got a flat tire.
3. a. He burned himself.
   b. He fainted.
4. a. Somebody stole his wallet.
   b. He got paint on his pants.
5. a. They fell on the sidewalk.
   b. They hurt themselves in the basement.
6. a. He fell in the water.
   b. He spilled the water.

READING

AN ACCIDENT

I saw an accident this morning while I was standing at the corner of Park Street and Central Avenue. A man in a small red sports car was driving down Park Street very fast. While he was driving, he was talking on his cell phone. At the same time, a woman in a large green pick-up truck was driving along Central Avenue very slowly. While she was driving, she was drinking a cup of coffee and eating a donut. While the woman was driving through the intersection, the man in the sports car didn't stop at a stop sign, and he crashed into the pick-up truck. The man and the woman were very upset. While they were shouting at each other, the police came.* Fortunately, nobody was hurt badly.

* come – came

✓ READING *CHECK-UP*

TRUE, FALSE, OR MAYBE?

Answer True, False, or Maybe (if the answer isn't in the story).

1. The accident happened at the corner of Park Street and Central Avenue.
2. The man was driving a small green sports car.
3. While the woman was driving, she was talking on her cell phone.
4. The man likes donuts.
5. The sports car crashed into the truck.
6. The woman was driving to work.
7. The police came after the accident.

How About You?
Tell about an accident you saw:
Where were you?
What happened?
Was anybody hurt?

PRONUNCIATION *Did & Was*

Listen. Then say it.	Say it. Then listen.
What did he do?	How did he hurt himself?
Who did he go with?	Where did he fall?
What was he doing?	Where was she going?
Where was she driving?	Where did it happen?

Some people like to go places and do things by themselves. Others like to do things with family members and friends. How about you? Do you like to do things alone or with other people? Write about it in your journal.

GRAMMAR FOCUS

Past Continuous Tense

What	was	I he she it	doing?
	were	we you they	

I He She It	was	eating.
We You They	were	

Complete the sentences with the correct form of the verb.

bake	listen	read	take	watch

What was everybody doing at 8:00 last night?

1. Monica _was reading_ the newspaper.
2. Michael _was taking_ a shower.
3. My parents _were watching_ TV.
4. You _was listening_ to music.
5. My wife and I _were baking_ cookies.

Reflexive Pronouns

I	took a walk by	myself.
You		yourself.
He		himself.
She		herself.
It		itself.
We		ourselves.
You		yourselves.
They		themselves.

While-Clauses

I lost my wallet **while I was jogging.**
He cut himself **while he was shaving.**

Complete the sentences with a reflexive pronoun and the correct form of the verb.

give	make	open	play	slice	sit

6. My brother hurt _himself_ while he _was playing_ basketball.
7. I cut _myself_ while I _was opening_ a package.
8. My sister burned _herself_ while she _was making_ pancakes.
9. My son and I got paint all over _ourselves_ while we _were sitting_ on a bench in the park.
10. My cousins spilled water all over _themselves_ while they _were giving_ their dog a bath.
11. Dad, did you cut _yourself_ while you _were slicing_ carrots?

LIFE SKILLS • Reporting an emergency at home

1 CONVERSATION Calling 911

Practice conversations to report these emergencies.

A. Emergency operator.
B. ______________________
A. What's the address?
B. ______________________
A. What's your name?
B. ______________________
A. Telephone number?
B. ______________________
A. Okay. We'll be there right away.

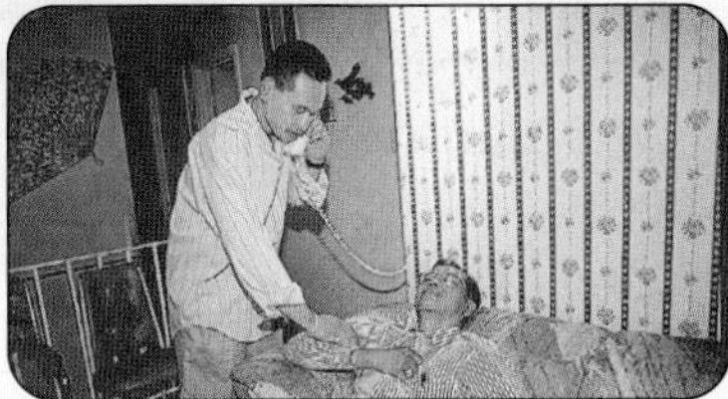

1. I think my father is having a heart attack!

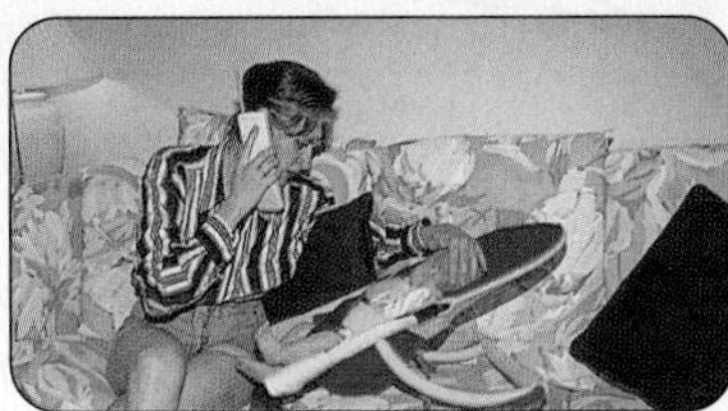

2. My baby is very sick! She isn't breathing!

3. There's a fire in my apartment building!

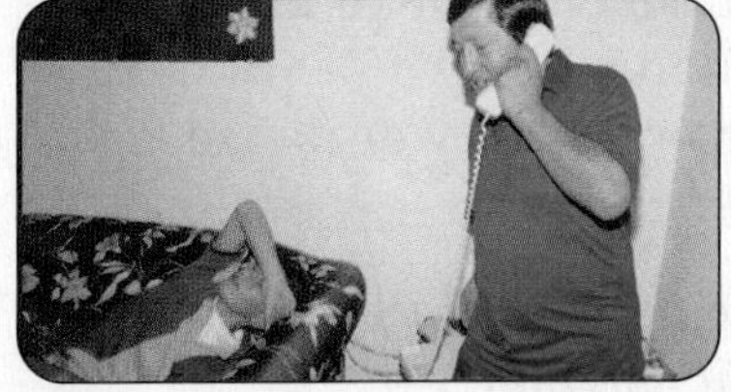

4. My son overdosed on some medicine! He isn't waking up!

5. Someone is breaking into my apartment!

6. There's a man with a gun in front of our building!

2 TEAMWORK Preparing for Emergencies at Home

Practice these interviews.

How are you prepared for an emergency at home?

I have a list of emergency numbers near the telephone.

I keep a first-aid kit in a convenient place.

I keep a fire extinguisher in my kitchen.

I change the batteries in my smoke detectors twice a year.

I know how to turn off the utilities.

I taught my children how to dial 911.

Now interview your classmates. Are they prepared for emergencies at home? Then discuss as a class: What else can you do to prepare for emergencies?

READING FIRST-AID INSTRUCTIONS

Look at the first-aid chart and answer the questions.

EMERGENCY FIRST AID	
Animal Bites: Wash the wound with soap and water for 5 minutes or more. Put a clean dry bandage on the wound. See a doctor as soon as possible. 	**Burns:** Cool the burn. Put it in cool water for 5 minutes or more. Do not use ice. Do not use any ointments or soap. Cover with a sterile dressing. 
Bee Stings: Try to remove the stinger with a clean knife. Clean the wound with soap and water and apply ice. Get medical help if the person is dizzy, nauseous, or can't breathe. 	**Choking:** If the person can speak, tell him or her to cough. If the person can't speak or cough, ask someone to call 911. Then get behind the person and perform the Heimlich maneuver. 
Bleeding: Apply direct pressure on the wound for 10 minutes with a clean cloth or a sterile dressing. If possible, raise the wound higher than the person's heart. 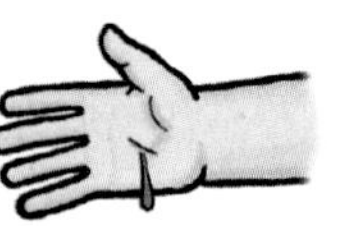	**Electric Shock:** Do not touch the person. Turn off the power. Call 911. If the person has no pulse, begin CPR (cardiopulmonary resuscitation). 

1. Perform the Heimlich maneuver when ____.
- A. someone is bleeding
- B. someone has an animal bite
- C. someone received an electric shock
- D. someone is choking

2. You should put ____ on a burn.
- A. ointment
- B. a sterile dressing
- C. ice
- D. soap

3. When someone is bleeding a lot, ____.
- A. try to remove the stinger
- B. clean the wound for 10 minutes
- C. apply pressure on the wound
- D. begin CPR

4. Wash ____ for 5 minutes or more.
- A. an animal bite
- B. a burn
- C. a bee sting
- D. a sterile dressing

5. Get medical help for a bee sting if ____.
- A. you don't have a clean knife
- B. the wound is dirty
- C. the person is dizzy or nauseous
- D. there isn't any ice

6. If someone gets an electric shock, DON'T ____.
- A. give the person CPR
- B. turn off the electricity
- C. call 911
- D. touch the person right away

READING A WARNING LABEL ON A HOUSEHOLD PRODUCT

DANGER: Avoid contact with eyes or skin. Wash thoroughly with soap after handling. Harmful if swallowed. Do not breathe vapors or fumes.

First-Aid Treatment: If swallowed, give a glassful of water or milk and call a Poison Control Center immediately. If in eyes, rinse with water for 15 minutes. Get medical attention. If on skin, wash with soap and water.

KEEP OUT OF REACH OF CHILDREN.

Decide if these sentences are True (T) or False (F).

____ **1.** Do not get this product in your eyes or on your hands, face, or other parts of your body.

____ **2.** Wash carefully with soap before you use this product.

____ **3.** It's dangerous to eat or drink this product.

____ **4.** Close the windows when you use this product.

____ **5.** Call the Poison Control Center if someone eats or drinks this product.

____ **6.** See a doctor if this product gets in your eyes.

Read the safety posters and answer the questions.

Duck, Cover, and Hold!
What to Do During an Earthquake

IN THE CLASSROOM:

Duck! Get down under a desk or table and drop to your knees. Turn away from the windows. Avoid heavy objects, like bookcases, that might fall.

Cover! Cover your head with the desk or table. Cover your eyes. (Put your face into your arm.)

Hold! Hold on to the desk or table. If it starts to move, hold on, move with it, and keep it over your head.

OUTSIDE: Find an area without buildings or trees. Stay away from electrical wires and poles on the ground. Get down on your knees and cover your head with a book or other object.

NEAR A BUILDING: Duck! Get into a doorway. Get down on your knees. Cover your head with one hand. Hold on to the doorway.

IN THE HALL: Duck down on the floor next to an inside wall and get on your knees. Cover your head and neck with your arms. Put your face down.

Preparing for a Hurricane

A hurricane watch means that a hurricane might arrive within 36 hours. When there is a hurricane watch, you should do the following:

- Have an emergency evacuation plan. If you have to evacuate, where will you go, and how will you get there?
- Have an emergency kit ready to take with you. It should contain a first-aid kit, flashlights and batteries, prescription medicine, sleeping bags, important documents, cash and credit cards, a non-electric can opener, and enough canned food, water, and clothes for five days.
- Listen to the radio or TV for weather reports and evacuation instructions.
- Fill your car with gas.
- Cover windows and doors with wood or tape.
- Move trash cans, bicycles, barbecue grills, and other objects inside or secure them so they'll stay in place during strong winds.
- Fill clean bottles and other containers with water for drinking.
- Fill sinks and bathtubs with water for washing.

1. If you're in the classroom during an earthquake, ____.

A. get under a bookcase
B. hold on to a window
C. cover your head with your knees
D. get under a desk or a table

2. If you're outside during an earthquake, ____.

A. get under a tree
B. look for a building
C. drop to your knees
D. get under an electrical pole

3. In the first instruction in the earthquake safety poster, *avoid* means ____.

A. cover
B. stay away from
C. stay near
D. hold on to

4. Evacuation instructions tell you ____.

A. what to do at home during a hurricane
B. how to prepare for a hurricane
C. what to do after a hurricane
D. what to do if you have to leave your home

5. You probably WON'T need ____ during a hurricane.

A. an electric can opener
B. a flashlight
C. canned food
D. drinking water

6. When there is a hurricane watch, you should NOT ____.

A. fill your car with gas
B. listen to the radio or TV
C. move bicycles and trash cans outside
D. fill sinks and bathtubs with water

ASSESSMENT • Check-up test • Self-evaluation checklists

Choose the correct answer.

1. Careful! Don't ____ yourself!
- A. spill
- B. hurt
- C. put
- D. faint

2. I saw you while you were ____ the library.
- A. getting off
- B. walking off
- C. walking into
- D. getting on

3. I ____ all my packages while I was walking down the stairs.
- A. fell
- B. tripped
- C. bit
- D. dropped

4. I had a terrible day today. I ____ myself in the eye.
- A. poked
- B. poured
- C. fixed
- D. hurt

5. There was an accident at the intersection. A car ____ into a truck.
- A. fell
- B. crashed
- C. broke
- D. spilled

6. I change the batteries in my ____ twice a year.
- A. first-aid kit
- B. utilities
- C. fire extinguishers
- D. smoke detectors

7. I always look at the ____ on a household product.
- A. first aid
- B. wound
- C. warning label
- D. bandage

8. If someone eats or drinks this product, call the ____ Control Center.
- A. Heimlich
- B. Poison
- C. CPR
- D. 911

9. In the classroom during an earthquake, get under your desk and ____ your eyes.
- A. duck
- B. move
- C. get on
- D. cover

10. I have flashlights in my emergency ____.
- A. kit
- B. report
- C. medicine
- D. watch

SKILLS CHECK ☑

Words:
- ☐ attend
- ☐ bite
- ☐ break into
- ☐ burn *myself*
- ☐ crash into
- ☐ cut *myself*
- ☐ deliver
- ☐ drop
- ☐ faint
- ☐ fall
- ☐ get a flat tire
- ☐ get off
- ☐ get on
- ☐ get out of
- ☐ hurt *myself*
- ☐ lose
- ☐ open
- ☐ poke *myself*
- ☐ practice
- ☐ spill
- ☐ stop
- ☐ take a test
- ☐ take a walk
- ☐ trip

I can ask & answer:
- ☐ What were we/you/they doing?
  We/You/They were working.
- ☐ What was he/she/it doing?
  He/She/It was working.
- ☐ Who did I/he/she/we/you/they go with?
  I went by myself./He went by himself./
  She went by herself./We went by ourselves./
  You went by yourself./You went by yourselves./
  They went by themselves.
- ☐ What happened?

I can react to bad news:
- ☐ I'm sorry to hear that.
- ☐ That's too bad!
- ☐ That's terrible!
- ☐ That's a shame!
- ☐ What a shame!
- ☐ What a pity!
- ☐ How awful!

I can:
- ☐ call 911 to report an emergency at home
- ☐ identify ways to prepare for emergencies at home

I can interpret:
- ☐ first-aid instructions
- ☐ warning labels on household products
- ☐ safety procedures for earthquakes and hurricanes

I can write about:
- ☐ doing things alone or with other people

10

Could
Be Able to
Have Got to
Too + Adjective

- Expressing Past and Future Ability
- Expressing Past and Future Obligation
- Giving an Excuse
- Renting an Apartment
- Housing Ads
- Reading a Floor Plan
- Requesting Maintenance and Repairs
- Building Rules and Regulations

VOCABULARY PREVIEW

1. busy
2. disappointed
3. frustrated
4. full
5. nervous
6. shy
7. sick
8. tired
9. upset
10. weak
11. crowded
12. difficult
13. heavy
14. spicy
15. windy

They Couldn't

I
He
She
It
We
You
They
} could / couldn't study.

Could he study?
Yes, he could.
No, he couldn't.

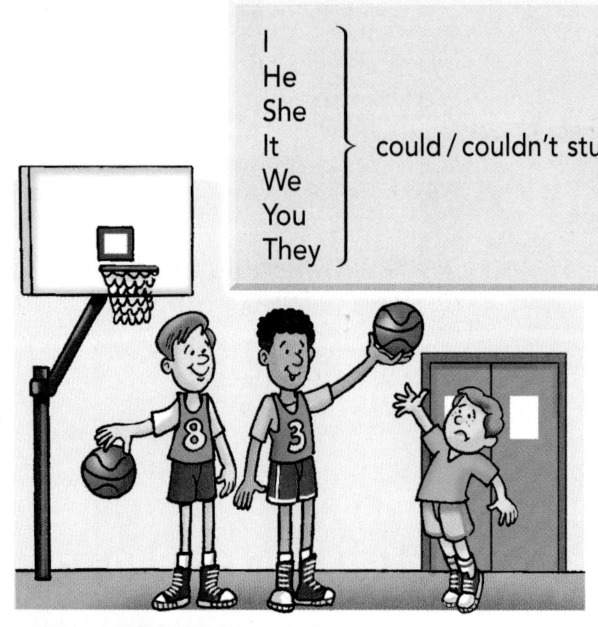

A. Could Peter play on the basketball team when he was a little boy?

B. No, he couldn't. He was too short.

1. Could Lisa go to lunch with her co-workers today?
busy

2. Could Sasha finish his homework last night?
tired

3. Could Max and Ruth finish their dinner yesterday?
full

4. Could you and your brother go to school yesterday?
sick

5. Could you walk the day after your operation?
weak

6. Could Timmy get into the movie last night?
young

7. Could Ben tell the police officer about the accident?
upset

8. Could Rita perform in school plays when she was young?
shy

9. Could Stuart and Gloria eat at their wedding?
nervous

They Weren't Able to

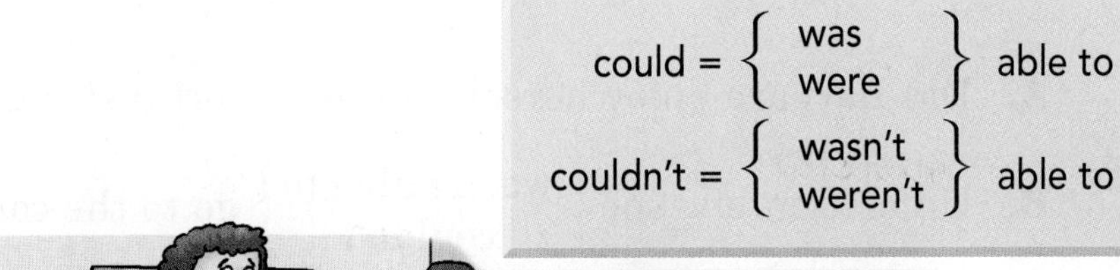

could = { was / were } able to
couldn't = { wasn't / weren't } able to

A. Was Jimmy able to lift his grandmother's suitcase?

B. No, he wasn't able to. It was too **heavy**.

1. Was Diane able to sit down on the subway this morning?
crowded

2. Was Charlie able to eat the food at the restaurant last night?
spicy

3. Were Nancy and Mark able to go camping last weekend?
windy

4. Were you able to solve the math problem last night?
difficult

5. Was Cathy able to find her cat last night?
dark

6. Were your parents able to swim in the ocean during their vacation?
cold

7. Was Tracy able to put her hair in a ponytail?
short

8. Was Ricky able to wear his brother's tuxedo to the prom?
small

She Had to Study for an Examination

A. Did Barbara enjoy herself at the concert last night?

B. Unfortunately, she { wasn't able to / couldn't } go to the concert last night. She had to **study for an examination**.

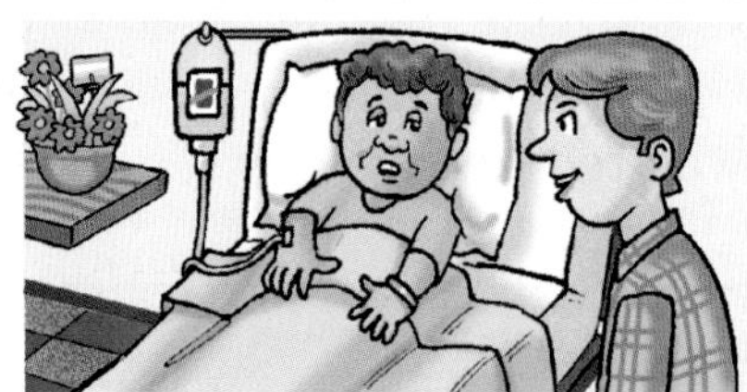

1. Did Paul enjoy himself at the tennis match last week?
visit his boss in the hospital

2. Did Amanda enjoy herself at the soccer game yesterday afternoon?
go to the eye doctor

3. Did you and your co-workers enjoy yourselves at the movies last night?
work overtime

4. Did Mr. and Mrs. Lee enjoy themselves at the symphony yesterday?
wait for the plumber

5. Did you enjoy yourself at the picnic last weekend?
work on my science project

6. Did Ralph enjoy himself at the amusement park last Sunday?
fix a flat tire

7. Did Carla enjoy herself at the school dance last Saturday night?
baby-sit for her neighbors

8.

READING

MRS. MURPHY'S STUDENTS COULDN'T DO THEIR HOMEWORK

Mrs. Murphy doesn't know what to do with her students today. They didn't do their homework last night, and now she can't teach the lesson she prepared.

Bob couldn't do his homework because he had a stomachache. Sally couldn't do her homework because she was tired and fell asleep early. John couldn't do his homework because he had to visit his grandmother in the hospital. Donna couldn't do her homework because she had to take care of her baby sister while her mother worked late at the office. And all the other students couldn't do their homework because there was a blackout in their neighborhood last night.

All the students promise Mrs. Murphy they'll be able to do their homework tonight. She certainly hopes so.

✓ READING *CHECK-UP*

Q & A

Mrs. Murphy is asking her students about their homework. Using this model, create dialogs based on the story.

A. *Bob*? Where's your homework?
B. I'm sorry, Mrs. Murphy. I couldn't do it.
A. You couldn't? Why not?
B. *I had a stomachache.*
A. Will you do your homework tonight?
B. Yes. I promise.

LISTENING

Listen and choose the correct answer.

1. a. It was too noisy.
   b. It was too crowded.
2. a. It was too windy.
   b. It was too upset.
3. a. It was too tired.
   b. It was too dark.
4. a. It was too full.
   b. It was too spicy.
5. a. They were too busy.
   b. They were too difficult.
6. a. I was too sick.
   b. I was too small.

I'm Afraid I Won't Be Able to Help You

will / won't be able to

(I have)	I've	got to work.
(We have)	We've	
(You have)	You've	
(They have)	They've	
(He has)	He's	
(She has)	She's	
(It has)	It's	

A. I'm afraid I won't be able to help you **move to your new apartment** tomorrow.

B. You won't? Why not?

A. I've got to **take my son to the doctor**.

B. Don't worry about it! I'm sure I'll be able to **move to my new apartment** by myself.

1. *paint your apartment*
   drive my parents to the airport

2. *repair your fence*
   take care of my niece and nephew

3. *study for the math test*
go to football practice

4. *set up your new computer*
fly to Denver

5. *hook up your new VCR*
take my daughter to her ballet lesson

6. *assemble Bobby's bicycle*
work late at the mall

7. *take Rover to the vet*
visit my mother in the hospital

8.

How to Say It!

Expressing obligation

A. { I've got to / I have to / I need to } *take my son to the doctor.*

B. Don't worry about it.

Practice the conversations in this lesson again. Express obligation in different ways.

READING

THE BATHROOM PIPE IS BROKEN

Mr. and Mrs. Wilson are very frustrated. A pipe broke in their bathroom yesterday while Mr. Wilson was taking a shower. They called the plumber, but she couldn't come yesterday. She was sick. She can't come today either. She's too busy. And, unfortunately, she won't be able to come tomorrow because tomorrow is Sunday, and she doesn't work on Sundays. Mr. and Mrs. Wilson are afraid they won't be able to use their shower for quite a while. That's why they're so frustrated.

THE TELEVISION IS BROKEN

Timmy Brown and his brother and sister are very frustrated. Their television broke yesterday while they were watching their favorite TV program. Their parents called the TV repairperson, but he couldn't come yesterday. He was fixing televisions on the other side of town. He can't come today either. His repair truck is broken. And, unfortunately, he won't be able to come tomorrow because he'll be out of town. Timmy Brown and his brother and sister are afraid they won't be able to watch TV for quite a while. That's why they're so frustrated.

✓ READING *CHECK-UP*

ANSWER THESE QUESTIONS

1. Could the plumber come to the Wilsons' house yesterday? Why not?
2. Can she come to their house today? Why not?
3. Will she be able to come to their house tomorrow? Why not?
4. Could the TV repairperson come to the Browns' house yesterday? Why not?
5. Can he come to their house today? Why not?
6. Will he be able to come to their house tomorrow? Why not?

CHOOSE

Mr. Wilson is calling the plumber again. Choose the correct words and then practice the conversation.

A. Hello. This is Mr. Wilson. You (have to got to)[1] send someone to fix our bathroom pipe. I've (have to got to)[2] take a shower!

B. I'm sorry, Mr. Wilson. You've (have to got to)[3] understand. We (can't aren't)[4] able to send a plumber right now. I (have to have)[5] a big job to do on the other side of town, and my assistant (has has to)[6] got to help me. We won't (can't be able to)[7] come over for a few more days.

ON YOUR OWN *Frustrated, Disappointed, and Upset*

Martha is upset. She got a flat tire, and she won't be able to get to the airport on time.

Frank is frustrated. He lost his key, and he can't get into his apartment.

Emily is upset. Her computer crashed, and she lost all her work. Now she won't be able to hand in her term paper tomorrow.

Ted was really disappointed last year. He couldn't dance in the school play. His teacher said he was too clumsy.

Are you frustrated, disappointed, or upset about something? Talk about it with other students in your class.

Think about a time you were frustrated, disappointed, or upset about something. What was the problem? How did you feel about it? What did you do about it? Write about it in your journal.

PRONUNCIATION *Have to & Have got to*

Listen. Then say it.	Say it. Then listen.
I have to work.	We have to study.
He has to go.	She has to leave.
They've got to wait.	You've got to practice.
He's got to eat.	She's got to drive.

GRAMMAR FOCUS

Could

Could	I he she it we you they	go?

Yes,	I he she it we you they	could.

No,	I he she it we you they	couldn't.

Be Able to

Was	I he she it	able to go?
Were	we you they	

No,	I he she it	wasn't	able to.
	we you they	weren't	

I'll He'll She'll It'll We'll You'll They'll	be able to help you.

I He She It We You They	won't be able to help you.

Have Got to

(I have) (We have) (You have) (They have)	I've We've You've They've	got to work.
(He has) (She has) (It has)	He's She's It's	

Too + Adjective

He was **too short**.
She was **too busy**.

Complete the sentences with the correct words.

able to	be able to	couldn't	got to	wasn't	won't

1. I won't be able to help you fix your car tomorrow.
2. My daughter couldn't go to school. She was too sick.
3. Mr. and Mrs. Ortega weren't able to go to the concert.
4. Alex wasn't able to finish his homework last night.
5. I've got to work overtime today.
6. I'm sure I'll be able to fix my computer by myself.

1 CONVERSATION Inquiring About Rentals

Practice conversations in an apartment rental office.

A. I'm looking for a _____ *-bedroom apartment.

B. We have a _____ *-bedroom apartment available.

A. Great. How much is the rent?

B. The rent is $_____ a month.

A. Does that include utilities?

B. Yes, it does. / No, it doesn't.

A. ______________________________

B. ______________________________
Would you like to see the apartment?

A. Yes, please.

* number of bedrooms

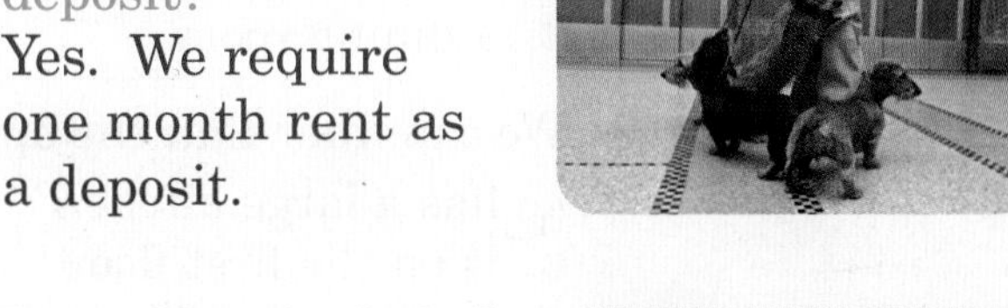

1. Is there a security deposit?
   Yes. We require one month rent as a deposit.

2. Are pets allowed in the building?
   Cats and small dogs are allowed. Large dogs are not permitted.

3. Is parking included in the rent?
   No. You have to pay extra for parking.

4. Is there public transportation nearby?
   Yes. There's a bus stop in front of the building.

TEAMWORK Work with a classmate. Make a list of other questions to ask about an apartment. Practice more conversations using these questions.

2 CONVERSATION Requesting Maintenance & Repairs

Practice with a classmate. Call about these apartment problems and others.

A. Hello. This is _____________ in apartment _____. I have a problem in my apartment.

B. What's the problem?

A. ______________________________

B. Okay. We'll send someone to fix it.

A. Thank you.

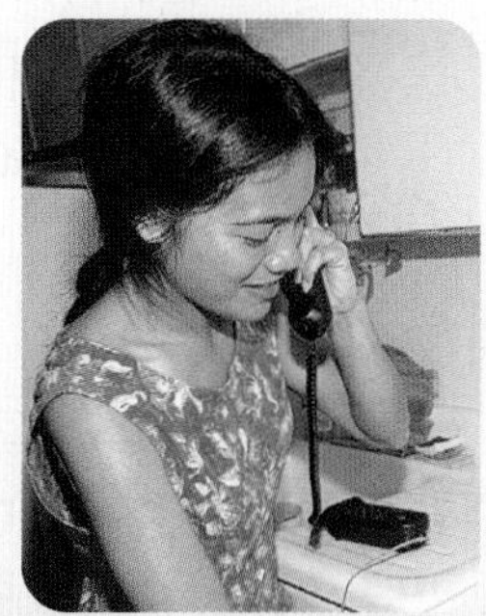

1. The stove doesn't turn on.
2. The refrigerator isn't working.
3. The dishwasher is leaking.
4. The kitchen sink is clogged.
5. The toilet keeps running.
6. ______________________________
7. ______________________________

READING HOUSING ADS

Look at the housing ads. Do you know all the abbreviations? Work with a classmate and read the ads aloud. Then answer the questions.

ARLINGTON Sunny 2 BR apt. Lg. eat-in kit., 1.5 BA, 3rd flr. mod. bldg. w/ elev. & washer/dryer. Pkg. for 2 cars. $900. Gas heat and hot water incl. Avail. June 16. Call landlord. 812-356-9872.	DANBURY 2 BR apt. in 2 fam. hse. Din. rm., lg. liv. rm., 1.5 BA, washer/dryer in bsmt. Pkg. on street. Nr. Danbury Park and #3 Bus. $700 mo. plus util. Call owner. 812-897-2469.
BAYSIDE 3 BR apt. w/ balc. on quiet st. Liv. rm., din. rm., 2.5 BA, kit. w/ new appliances. Walk to stores. Avail. immed. $875 mo. Call bldg. mgr. 812-724-0968.	DEARING Beaut. 3 BR apt. New refrig. & d/w. in kit., 2 BA, a/c. Laundry rm. in bsmt. Nr. excel. schls. Avail. 7/1. $900 mo. Call supt. 812-497-2741.

1. If you want to rent the apartment in Dearing, you should call the ____.
   A. building manager
   B. superintendent
   C. landlord

2. The apartment in Arlington has ____.
   A. three bedrooms
   B. a small kitchen
   C. one and a half bathrooms

3. You can move into the apartment in ____ right away.
   A. Arlington
   B. Bayside
   C. Dearing

4. You don't have to pay extra for heat if you rent the apartment in ____.
   A. Arlington
   B. Danbury
   C. Dearing

5. The apartment in Danbury does NOT have ____.
   A. a garage
   B. a washing machine in the basement
   C. a dining room

6. We can infer that the apartment in Bayside ____.
   A. has a large kitchen
   B. is on the first floor
   C. has a new refrigerator

TEAMWORK **Cut out some housing ads from the newspaper and bring them to class. Work with a classmate. Compare ads for different places. What information do you see? List the abbreviations in the ads. Discuss which places you like and why.**

READING A FLOOR PLAN

Look at the floor plan. Decide if these sentences are True (T) or False (F).

____ 1. The apartment has three bedrooms.

____ 2. The apartment has five closets.

____ 3. One of the closets is in the dining room.

____ 4. There are one and a half bathrooms.

____ 5. There's a fireplace in the bedroom.

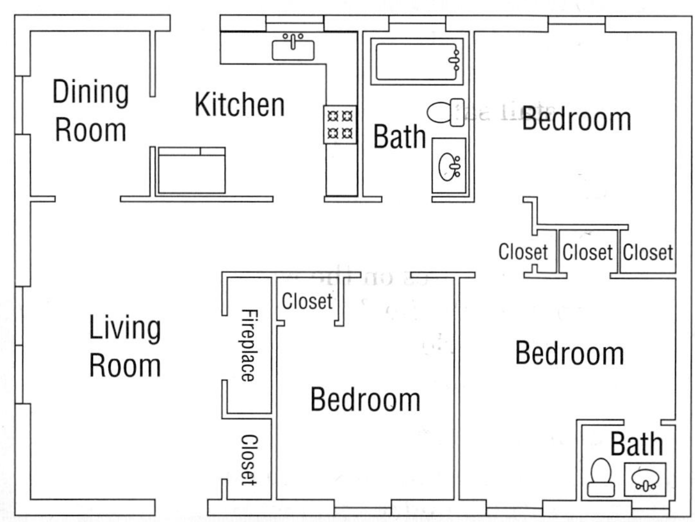

PROJECT **Draw a floor plan of your apartment or home. Show all the rooms, bathrooms, and closets. Then write a housing ad for your apartment or home, using abbreviations.**

LIFE SKILLS READING • Apartment building regulations

Read the apartment building regulations and answer the questions.

Building Rules and Regulations

Rent: Rent is due on or before the first day of each month. Pay with a check or a money order.

Noise: Do not make noise that disturbs other people in the building. There will be no noisy parties or loud playing of radios, stereos, musical instruments, or TVs, especially between 10 P.M. and 8 A.M.

Security: Do not give guests the key to your apartment. Do not let non-tenants who you do not know into the building. When you leave the building, lock the door to your apartment. Tell the building manager if your apartment is going to be empty for more than five days.

Health and Safety: Keep your apartment safe and clean. Keep hallways, stairs, laundry room, and other common areas clear. You can store bicycles and other personal belongings in the storage room in the basement.

Smoke Detectors/Bathroom Fans: Do not disconnect smoke detectors or bathroom fans. Tell the building manager when there is a problem with a smoke detector. If we find a smoke detector that isn't working, we will repair it and charge you for the repair.

Laundry: The laundry room is for residents only. It is open from 8 A.M. to 9:30 P.M. Remove all laundry from machines promptly, and keep the laundry area neat and clean.

Pets: There will be no pets in any of the apartments.

Balconies: Do not hang laundry or keep boxes, trash, or other items on your balcony. For safety reasons, do not use a barbecue grill on the balcony.

Parking: Park in the parking spaces provided for you and your guests. There is no parking on the grass or in the driveway.

Satellite Dishes/TV Antennas: Do not install satellite dishes or TV antennas without asking the landlord.

Hanging Items: Use small nails or picture hangers to hang items on the walls.

Changes to Rules and Regulations: We have the right to change these rules and regulations at any time.

1. Tenants have to ______.
- A. store their bicycles in the hallway
- B. park in the driveway
- C. install satellite dishes or antennas
- D. pay rent with a check or money order

2. Tenants have to ask the landlord before they can ______.
- A. hang pictures on the walls
- B. install satellite dishes
- C. store bicycles
- D. let someone into the building

3. Tenants can ______.
- A. store books in the basement
- B. use the laundry room at 10 P.M.
- C. change the rules and regulations
- D. store boxes on their balconies

4. Tenants should ______ when they leave the building.
- A. tell the building manager
- B. disconnect bathroom fans
- C. lock their doors
- D. give the building manager their keys

5. It is unsafe to ______.
- A. hang items on the walls
- B. remove laundry from machines promptly
- C. keep common areas clear
- D. use barbecues on the balconies

6. In the sixth rule, the word *residents* refers to ______.
- A. laundry workers
- B. guests
- C. tenants
- D. employees

Choose the correct answer.

1. Nobody was able to ___ the math problem. It was too difficult.
   A. perform
   B. solve
   C. go
   D. have

2. I couldn't lift the box because it was too ___.
   A. weak
   B. tired
   C. light
   D. heavy

3. I'll be happy to help you ___ your new computer.
   A. hand in
   B. crash
   C. set up
   D. break

4. We couldn't sit down on the bus because it was too ___.
   A. frustrated
   B. crowded
   C. clumsy
   D. disappointed

5. Were you able to ___ your son's bicycle by yourself?
   A. get into
   B. hook up
   C. assemble
   D. baby-sit

6. We require one month rent as ___.
   A. a security deposit
   B. utilities
   C. extra
   D. available

7. The ___ in our apartment isn't working. We have to repair it.
   A. satellite dish
   B. laundry
   C. parking space
   D. smoke detector

8. If you make a lot of noise, you'll ___ other tenants in the building.
   A. disturb
   B. disconnect
   C. remove
   D. install

BRADBURY 1 BR apt. Kit. w/ new stove, lge. liv. rm., 1.5 BA, laundry rm. in bsmt. $750 mo. plus utilities. Parking on street. Avail. Sept 15. Call supt. 310-659-4581.

BRANFORD 3 BR apt. in mod. apt. bldg., 2 BA, lge. liv. rm., kit. w/ dishwasher. Garage. Walk to stores. $900 plus utils. Call bldg. mgr. 310-393-2277.

DEXTER 2 BR apt. 1 BA, liv. rm. w/ frplc., lge. din. rm., balc. No pkg. Nr. mall. $800. Utils. incl. Avail. immed. Call landlord. 310-274-9836.

Look at the apartment ads. Choose the correct answer.

9. According to the ad, the apartment in Branford has ___.
   A. a new stove in the kitchen
   B. a large dining room
   C. one and a half bathrooms
   D. parking

10. According to the ad, if you rent the two-bedroom apartment, ___.
    A. you'll have to pay extra for heat
    B. you'll have two bathrooms
    C. you can move in right away
    D. you'll have to pay extra for electricity

SKILLS CHECK ☑

Words:

☐ busy
☐ clumsy
☐ cold
☐ crowded
☐ dark
☐ difficult
☐ disappointed
☐ frustrated
☐ full
☐ heavy
☐ nervous
☐ short
☐ shy
☐ sick
☐ small
☐ spicy
☐ tired
☐ upset
☐ weak
☐ windy
☐ young
☐ apartment
☐ appliances
☐ balcony
☐ bathroom fan
☐ building manager
☐ hallway
☐ heat
☐ hot water
☐ landlord
☐ laundry room
☐ owner
☐ parking
☐ parking space
☐ personal belongings
☐ rent
☐ resident
☐ rules and regulations
☐ security deposit
☐ smoke detector
☐ storage room
☐ tenant
☐ utilities

I can ask & answer:

☐ Could you *go*?
  Yes, I could.
  No, I couldn't.
☐ Were you able to *go*?
  Yes, I was able to.
  No, I wasn't able to.
☐ How much is the rent?
☐ Does that include utilities?
☐ Is there a security deposit?
☐ Are pets allowed in the building?
☐ Is parking included in the rent?
☐ Is there public transportation nearby?

I can express obligation:

☐ I've got to/I have to/I need to *study*.

I can:

☐ inquire about apartment rentals
☐ request maintenance and repairs

I can interpret:

☐ housing ads
☐ a floor plan
☐ apartment building rules and regulations

I can write about:

☐ a problem I experienced

SIDE by SIDE Gazette

Volume 2 Number 4

Families and Time

Families have less time together

It seems that everywhere around the world, people are spending more time at work or alone and less time with their families and friends. People are busier than ever before!

In the past in many countries, the father worked and the mother stayed home, took care of the children, and did the food shopping, cooking, and cleaning. Nowadays in many families, both parents work, so they both have to do the shopping, cooking, and cleaning in their free time. Parents, therefore, don't have as much time with their children as they used to have in the past. There are also many single-parent families. In these families, the single parent has to do everything.

These days, many children come home from school to an empty apartment or house. A lot of children spend many hours each day in front of the television. Even when families are together, it is common for family members to do things by themselves. For example, they watch programs on separate TVs in different rooms, they use the Internet, they talk with friends on the telephone, and they do other individual activities.

Isn't it strange? Thanks to technology, people are able to communicate so easily with people far away, but sometimes they don't communicate as well as before with people in their own homes.

Is this happening in your country? What's your opinion about this?

FACT FILE

Countries Where People Spend the Most Time at Work

Country	Hours of Work Per Year
Thailand	2,200
United States	1,966
Japan	1,889
France	1,656
Germany	1,560

BUILD YOUR VOCABULARY!

Home Appliances

I think the ____ is broken!

- coffee maker

- dishwasher

- dryer

- garbage disposal

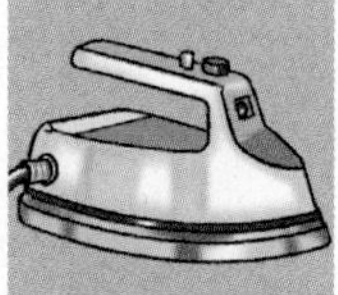

- iron

- microwave

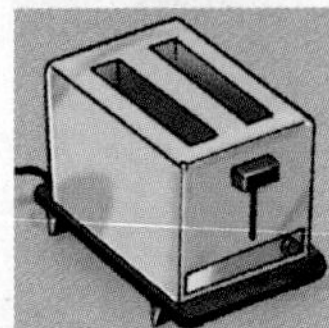

- toaster

- vacuum cleaner

- washing machine / washer

AROUND THE WORLD

Child Care

While parents around the world are working, who takes care of their young children? There are many different types of child care for pre-school children around the world.

These children are in a day-care center in their community.

These children are in a day-care center in a factory where their parents work.

This child stays home during the day with his grandmother.

What different types of child care are there in countries you know?

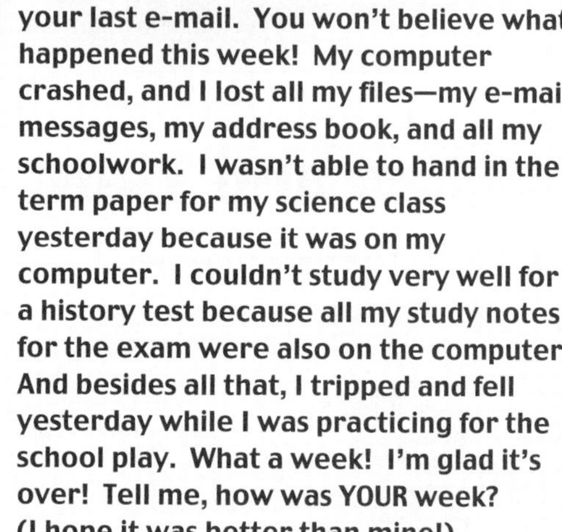

Global Exchange

KoolKid2: Hi. It's me. I'm sorry I didn't answer your last e-mail. You won't believe what happened this week! My computer crashed, and I lost all my files—my e-mail messages, my address book, and all my schoolwork. I wasn't able to hand in the term paper for my science class yesterday because it was on my computer. I couldn't study very well for a history test because all my study notes for the exam were also on the computer. And besides all that, I tripped and fell yesterday while I was practicing for the school play. What a week! I'm glad it's over! Tell me, how was YOUR week? (I hope it was better than mine!)

Send a message to a keypal. Tell a little about your week.

LISTENING

You have five messages!

You Have Five Messages!

d	1 Pete has to	a.	fix his car.
e	2 Susie has to	b.	stay in bed.
a	3 Marty has to	c.	wait for the plumber.
c	4 Judy has to	d.	work overtime.
b	5 Tom had to	e.	visit her grandparents.

What Are They Saying?

11

Past Tense Review
Count/Non-Count Noun Review
Must
Mustn't vs. Don't Have to
Must vs. Should

- Medical Examinations
- Medical Advice
- Health
- Nutrition
- Making a Doctor Appointment
- Calling in Sick
- Reporting Absence from School
- Medicine Labels
- Medicine Safety Tips
- Nutrition and Recipes

VOCABULARY PREVIEW

1 
2 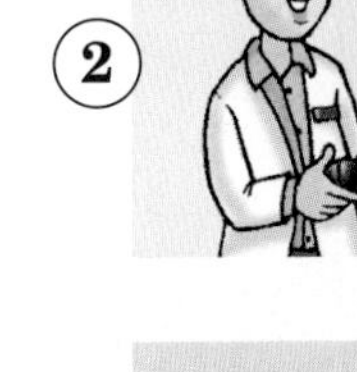
3 
4 
5 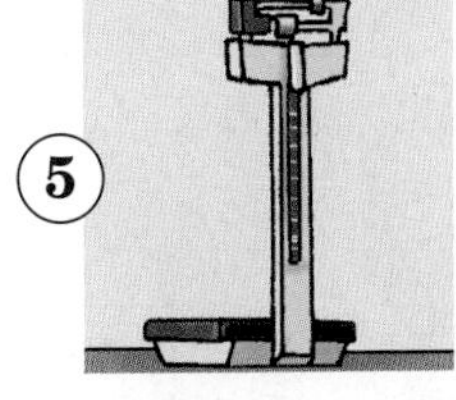
6 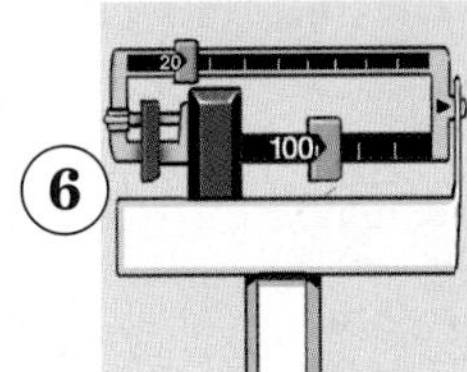

7 
8 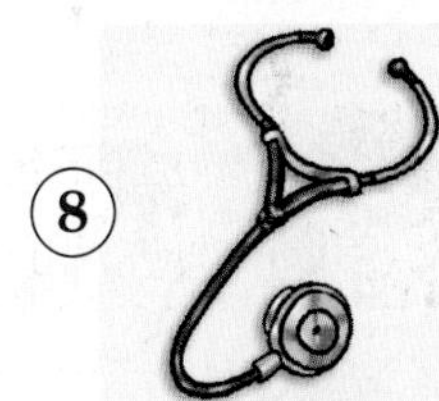
9 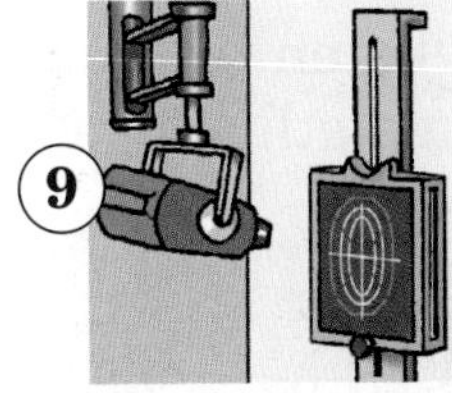
10 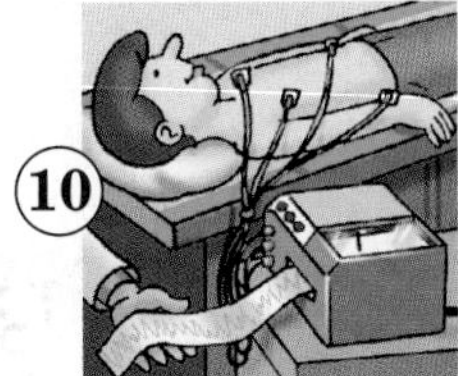
11 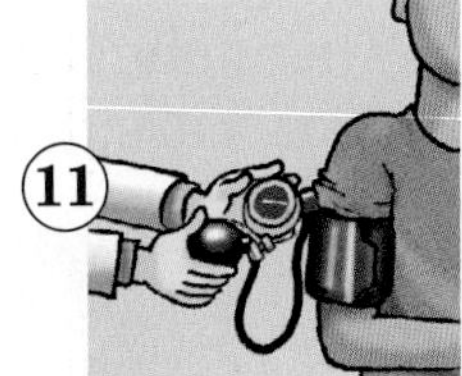
12 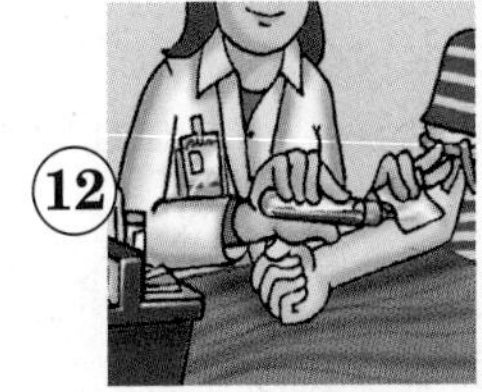

1. doctor
2. nurse
3. lab technician
4. X-ray technician
5. scale
6. weight
7. height
8. stethoscope
9. chest X-ray
10. cardiogram
11. blood pressure
12. blood test

The Checkup

You'll stand* on a scale, and the nurse will measure your height and your weight.

The nurse will take your blood pressure.

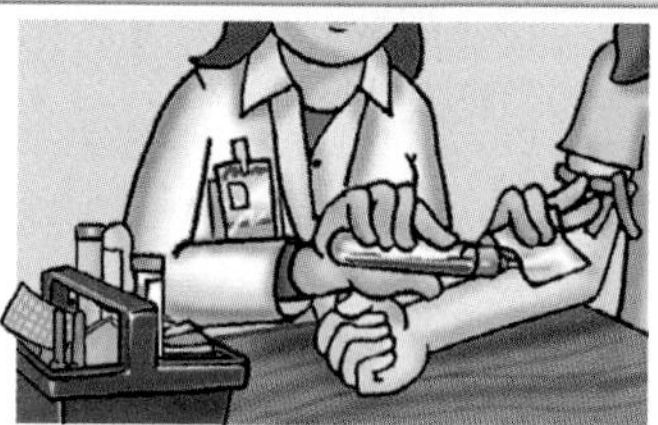

The lab technician will do some blood tests.

The X-ray technician will take a chest X-ray.

Then the nurse will lead* you into an examination room.

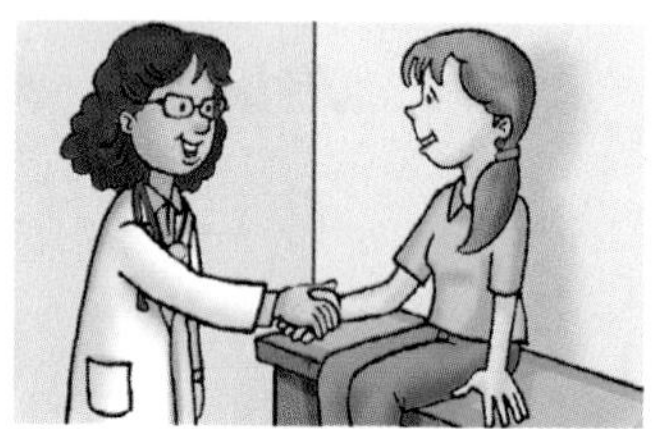

The doctor will come in, shake* your hand, and say "hello."

She'll ask you some questions about your health.

Then, she'll examine your eyes, ears, nose, and throat.

Next, she'll listen to your heart with a stethoscope.

After that, she'll take your pulse.

Then, she'll do a cardiogram.

Finally, the doctor will talk with you about your health.

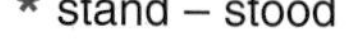

* stand – stood   lead – led   shake – shook

Your Checkup

1. I stood on a scale and the nurse measured my heigh and my weight

2. The nurse took my blood pressure

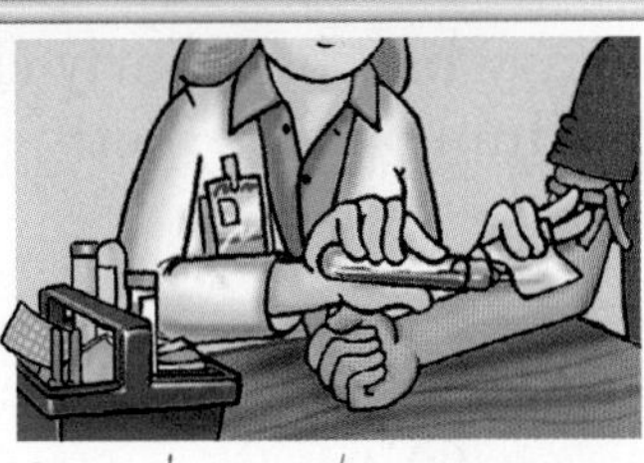

3. The lab technician did some blood test

4. The X-Ray technician took a chest X Ray

5. Then nurse led you into an examination room

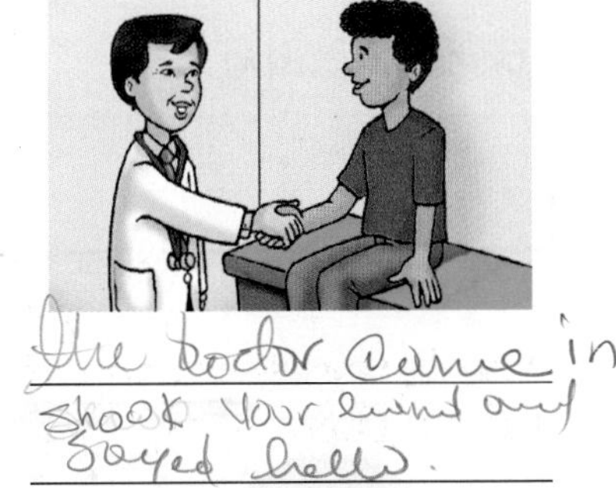

6. The doctor came in shook your hand and sayed hello.

7. He asked you some question about your health

8. Then he examined your eyes ears, nose, and throat.

9. Next, he listened to your heart with a stethoscope

10. After, that he'll took my pulse

11. Then, he did a cardiogram

12. finally The doctor

Diets

I He She It We You They	must work.

more / less	more / fewer
bread	cookies
fish	potatoes
fruit	eggs
rice	vegetables

Henry had his yearly checkup today. The doctor told him he's a little too heavy and put him on this diet:

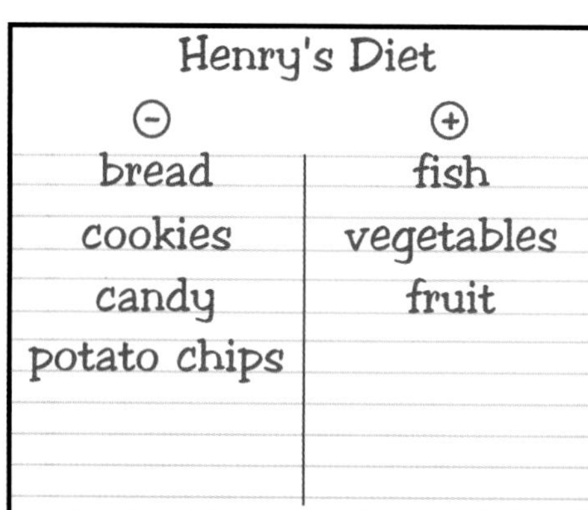

Henry's Diet

⊖	⊕
bread	fish
cookies	vegetables
candy	fruit
potato chips	

You must eat **less** bread, **fewer** cookies, **less** candy, and **fewer** potato chips. Also, you must eat **more** fish, **more** vegetables, and **more** fruit.

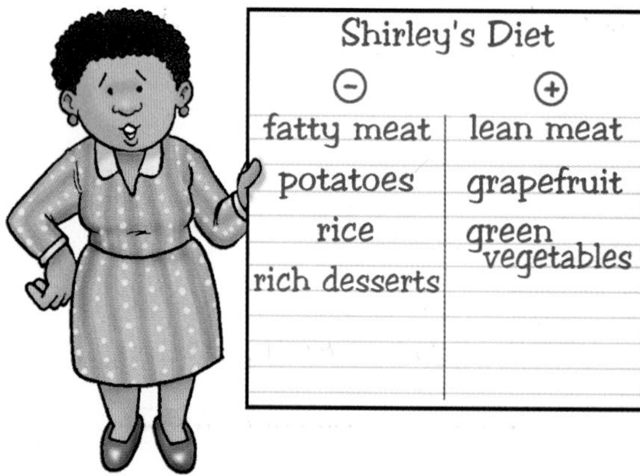

Shirley's Diet

⊖	⊕
fatty meat	lean meat
potatoes	grapefruit
rice	green vegetables
rich desserts	

Arthur's Diet

⊖	⊕
butter	margarine
eggs	yogurt
cheese	skim milk
ice cream	

1. Shirley also had her annual checkup today. The doctor told her she's a little too heavy and put her on this diet:

She must eat less fatty meat fewer potatoes less rice fewer rich desserts and she must eat more lean meat more grapefruit more green vegetables

2. Arthur was worried about his heart. He went to his doctor for an examination, and the doctor told him to eat fewer fatty foods.

He must eat/drink less butter fewer eggs less cheese, less ice cream, he must eat more margarine, more yogurt more skim milk.

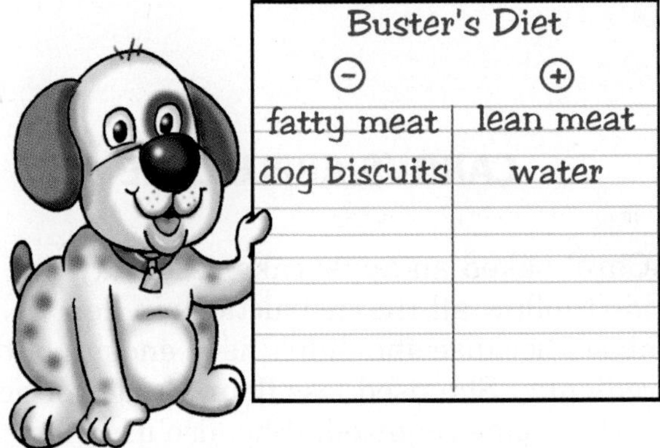

Buster's Diet
⊖ ⊕
fatty meat | lean meat
dog biscuits | water

My Diet

⊖	⊕

3. Buster went to the vet yesterday for his yearly checkup. The vet told him he's a little too heavy and put him on this diet:

   He must eat/drink less fatty meat fewer biscuits he must eat more lean must and drink more water.

4. You went to the doctor today for your annual physical examination. The doctor told you you're a little overweight and said you must go on a diet.

   I must eat/drink fewer cookies, less candy ______ .

LISTENING

Listen and choose the correct word to complete the sentence.

1. a. cake
   (b.) cookies
2. (a.) bread
   b. vegetables
3. (a.) soda
   b. grapefruit
4. a. rice
   (b.) desserts
5. (a.) fatty meat
   b. eggs
6. a. cheese
   (b.) potato chips

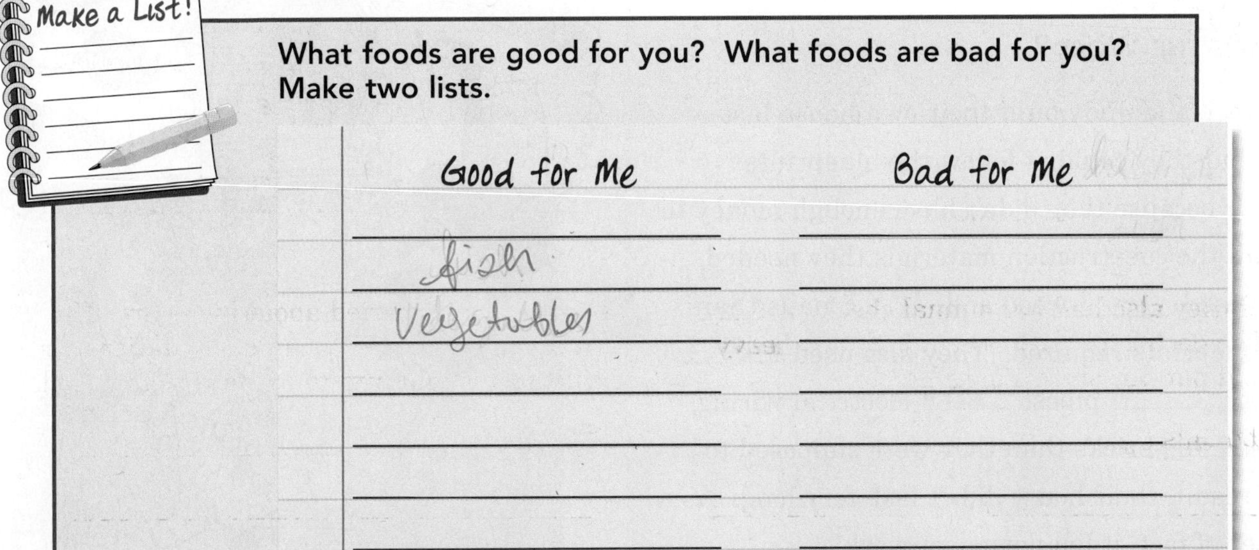

What foods are good for you? What foods are bad for you? Make two lists.

Good for Me	Bad for Me
fish	
Vegetables	

READING

CAROL'S APPLE CAKE

Carol baked an apple cake yesterday, but she couldn't follow all the instructions in her cookbook because she didn't have enough of the ingredients. She used less flour and fewer eggs than the recipe required. She also used less butter, fewer apples, fewer raisins, and less sugar than she was supposed to. As a result, Carol's apple cake didn't taste very good. As a matter of fact, it tasted terrible!

PAUL'S BEEF STEW

Paul cooked beef stew yesterday, but he couldn't follow all the instructions in his cookbook because he didn't have enough of the ingredients. He used less meat and fewer tomatoes than the recipe required. He also used fewer potatoes, less salt, less pepper, and fewer onions than he was supposed to. As a result, Paul's beef stew didn't taste very good. As a matter of fact, it tasted awful!

✓ READING *CHECK-UP*

WHAT'S THE WORD?

Steve and Judy built their own house last year, but they couldn't follow the blueprints exactly because they didn't have enough money to buy all the construction materials they needed. They used ______ 1 wood and ______ 2 nails than the blueprints required. They also used ______ 3 cement, ______ 4 pipes, ______ 5 electrical wiring, and ______ 6 bricks than they were supposed to. As a result, their house didn't last very long. As a matter of fact, it fell down last week!

They Must Lose Some Weight

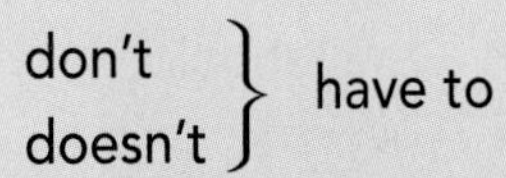

mustn't
(must not)
don't
doesn't
have to

A. I had my yearly checkup today.

B. What did the doctor say?

A. He said I'm a little too heavy and I must lose some weight.

B. Do you have to stop eating **ice cream**?

A. No. I don't have to stop eating **ice cream**. But I mustn't eat as much **ice cream** as I did before.

A. Grandpa had his yearly checkup today.

B. What did the doctor say?

A. She said he's a little too heavy and he must lose some weight.

B. Does he have to stop eating **cookies**?

A. No. He doesn't have to stop eating **cookies**. But he mustn't eat as many **cookies** as he did before.

1. I had my yearly checkup today.

2. Billy had his yearly checkup today.

3. Grandma had her yearly checkup today.

4. Rover had his yearly checkup today.

Really, Doctor?

should must

A. I'm really worried about your heart.

B. Really, Doctor? Should I stop eating rich desserts?

A. Mr. Jones! You MUST stop eating rich desserts! If you don't, you're going to have serious problems with your heart some day.

A. I'm really worried about your ________.

B. Really, Doctor? Should I ____________?

A. (Mr./Miss/Mrs./Ms.) ________! You MUST ____________! If you don't, you're going to have serious problems with your ________ some day.

1. *knees*
   stop jogging

2. *back*
   start doing exercises

3. *stomach*
   stop eating spicy foods

4. *blood pressure*
   take life a little easier

5. *hearing*
   stop listening to loud rock music

6.

How to Say It!

Asking for Advice

A. *I have a cold.* { What should I do? / Do you have any advice? / Do you have any suggestions? }

B. I think you should *drink some hot tea.*

Practice the conversations on this page, using these expressions for asking for advice.

INTERACTIONS

HOME REMEDIES

Different people have different remedies for medical problems that aren't very serious. For example, people do different things when they burn a finger.

Some people rub butter on their finger.

Other people put a piece of ice on their finger.

Other people put their finger under cold water.

Practice conversations with other students. Ask for advice about these medical problems, and give advice about "home remedies" you know.

I have a cold.
I have a toothache.
I have a stomachache.
I have a bloody nose.
I have the hiccups.

PRONUNCIATION *Must & Mustn't*

Listen. Then say it.

I must eat more fruit.

He must eat fewer cookies.

You mustn't eat cake.

They mustn't eat ice cream.

Say it. Then listen.

We must eat less cheese.

She must eat more vegetables.

I mustn't eat butter.

They mustn't eat potato chips.

There are a lot of rules in daily life—things you must do and things you mustn't do. Think about the rules in YOUR life—at school, on the job, in your home, and in your community. Write about these rules in your journal.

GRAMMAR FOCUS

MUST

I He She It We You They	must work.

I He She It We You They	mustn't eat candy.

MUSTN'T VS. DON'T HAVE TO

I **don't have to** stop eating cookies.
But I **mustn't** eat as many cookies as I did before.

MUST VS. SHOULD

Should I stop eating rich desserts?
You **must** stop eating rich desserts.

COUNT/NON-COUNT NOUNS:

NON-COUNT

He must eat	more less	bread. fish. meat.

COUNT

He must eat	more fewer	cookies. potatoes. eggs.

Choose the correct word.

1. I'm a little heavy. I know I (must mustn't) lose some weight.
2. You (must shouldn't) stop jogging. If you don't, you're going to have problems with your knees.
3. My doctor says I must eat (fewer less) eggs and (fewer less) butter.
4. You (must mustn't) eat as (many much) candy or as (many much) cookies as you did before.
5. I (don't have to must) stop eating ice cream, but I (have to mustn't) have it every day.
6. I know I should eat (fewer less) french fries, but I love them. My doctor says I (must mustn't) eat as many as I do now.
7. My husband has high blood pressure. I always tell him he (mustn't should) stop putting so (much many) salt on his food.
8. Michael's cookies didn't taste very good. He used (fewer less) flour and (fewer less) raisins than the recipe required. He knows that next time he (must mustn't) follow the recipe more carefully.

1 CONVERSATION MAKING A DOCTOR APPOINTMENT

Practice with a classmate. Make appointments for these medical problems. Use your name and any time you wish.

A. Doctor's office.

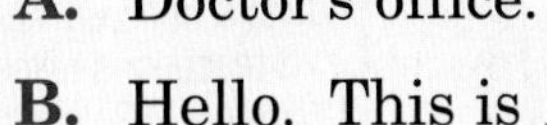

B. Hello. This is ___(first & last name)___.
I'd like to make an appointment.

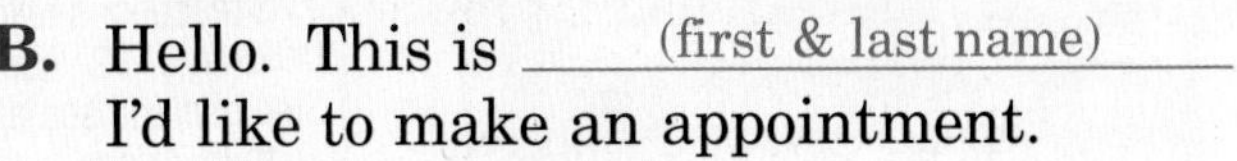

A. What's the problem?

B. I have a bad __________.

A. Can you come in tomorrow at ___(time)___?

B. Tomorrow at ___(time)___? Yes. Thank you.

1. stomachache

2. headache

3. backache

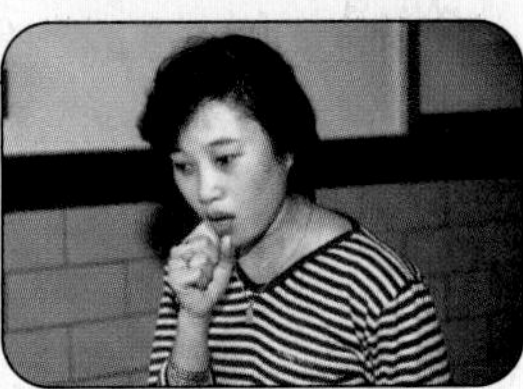

4. cough

5. earache

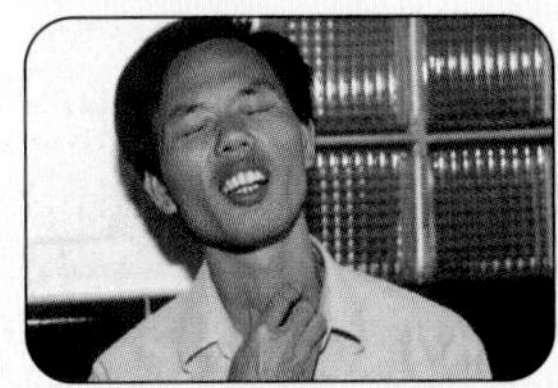

6. sore throat

7. fever

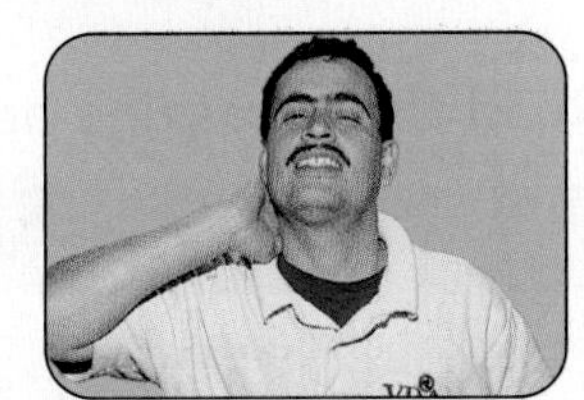

8. stiff neck

2 CONVERSATION CALLING IN SICK

Practice with a classmate.

A. Hello. This is ___(first & last name)___.
I'm sorry, but I can't come to work today. I'm sick.

B. I'm sorry to hear that. What's the matter?

A. __________________.

B. Okay. I hope you feel better soon.

A. Thank you.

3 CONVERSATION & WRITING REPORTING ABSENCE FROM SCHOOL

Practice with a classmate.

A. Hello. This is ___(first & last name)___.
My son/daughter ___(child's name)___
will be absent from school today.
He's/She's sick.

B. Okay. Thank you for calling.

Write a note to the teacher the next day.

___(date)___

Dear ___(teacher's name)___,

My son/daughter ___(name)___ was absent from school yesterday because __________.

Sincerely,

___(your name)___

Read the medicine labels. Decide if the sentences are True (T) or False (F).

BAXTER ASPIRIN
Directions: Drink a full glass of water with each dose.
Adults: Take 1 or 2 tablets every 4 hours or 3 tablets every 6 hours.
Ask a doctor before using if you have stomach problems.

Acutron Cough Syrup
Directions:
Adults & children 12 years of age and over: 2 teaspoons twice a day.
Children 6–12 years: 1 teaspoon twice a day.
Stop use and see a doctor if cough lasts more than 7 days.
WARNING: May cause drowsiness. Do not drive or operate equipment while taking this medicine.

LABOPROFIN
RX#47812
DATE: 6/15/11
ERIC ANDERSON
ONE CAPSULE EVERY 3 HOURS AS NEEDED FOR PAIN. TAKE WITH FOOD IF STOMACH UPSET OCCURS.
USE BEFORE 6/15/12.
DR. CHOU

____ **1.** You should stop taking Acutron Cough Syrup if your cough doesn't get better after seven days.
____ **2.** Dr. Chou wrote a prescription for Laboprofin on June fifteenth, 2012.
____ **3.** An adult can take three Baxter Aspirin tablets every four hours.
____ **4.** Eleven-year old children can take two teaspoons of Acutron Cough Syrup a day.
____ **5.** When you take two Baxter Aspirin tablets you should drink a glass of water.
____ **6.** Eric Anderson should stop taking Laboprofin if he gets a stomachache.

Read the magazine article. Decide if the sentences are True (T) or False (F).

Medicine Safety Tips

Pharmacies have many aisles of medicine for every kind of ailment. There are decongestants and nose drops for stuffy noses, throat lozenges for sore throats, aspirin and other pain relievers for headaches, antihistamines for allergies, and antacids for stomachaches. Although you don't need a prescription for any of these over-the-counter drugs, they can hurt you if don't use them correctly.

Before you take a non-prescription medicine, be sure to read the label carefully. The label tells you what the medicine is for, its ingredients, the correct dosage (how much to take and how often), and the expiration date. If you take two or more medicines at the same time, read the labels carefully to make sure you don't take too much of an ingredient. Throw away the medicine if it is past the expiration date.

The warning on the label tells you when *not* to use the medicine, when to stop taking it, and possible problems or side effects you might have such as stomach pains. This information can help you decide if this is the right medicine for you. If you don't understand the label, talk to the pharmacist or your doctor. If you take the medicine and you don't feel better, see a doctor. You might have a more serious health problem that requires stronger medication.

Your doctor might write a prescription for medicine you will get at a pharmacy. Tell the doctor about any other medications you are taking because it can be dangerous to mix medicines. Prescription medicine has more possible side effects than over-the-counter medicine, so it's especially important to understand the directions and warnings on the label and to ask your doctor and pharmacist questions.

____ **1.** Antihistamines are for stomachaches.
____ **2.** Doctors prescribe over-the-counter drugs.
____ **3.** Non-prescription medicine isn't as strong as prescription medicine.
____ **4.** It's good to mix medicines.
____ **5.** Dosage instructions tell you how many times a day to take the medicine.
____ **6.** Stomachaches are a possible side effect.
____ **7.** The warning on the label tells you what the medicine is for.

Read the magazine article and answer the questions.

A Healthy Diet

Are you overweight? Do you feel tired all the time? Eating healthier foods will give you energy and will help you lose those extra pounds. It will also protect you from high blood pressure, heart problems, and other diseases.

Eat small amounts of many different kinds of food each day. It's important to eat food that is high in vitamins, minerals, and other nutrients and low in sugar, salt, and unhealthy fats. Eat fruits, vegetables, whole grains (whole wheat bread, brown rice, whole grain cereal), and low-fat dairy products (low-fat milk, low-fat yogurt). These foods provide most of the vitamins and minerals that you need, such as calcium and potassium. Include protein in your diet. You can get protein from meat, chicken, fish, eggs, beans, and nuts. Protein is important, but you should eat more fruits, vegetables, grains, and dairy products than protein.

Most of the fat you eat should come from fish, nuts, and vegetable oil. Fat from meat, chicken, butter, margarine, cream, mayonnaise, fried foods, and snack foods is bad for your heart.

Lemon Chicken

Ingredients

1 chicken, cut up
2 Tbsp. vegetable oil
2 Tbsp. lemon juice
1 tsp. mustard
pepper

Tbsp.= tablespoon
tsp.= teaspoon

Place the chicken in a baking pan. Mix the vegetable oil, mustard, and lemon juice and pour it over the chicken. Add pepper to taste. Bake at 375° for 45 minutes.

Buy fish or lean meat. If there is fat on the meat, cut off the fat before you cook it. For example, cook chicken without the skin. Don't cook with a lot of oil. It's better to grill, broil, or microwave food than to fry it.

Sugar doesn't have any nutrients, and it's bad for your teeth. Drink water or diet soda instead of soda, and eat very few sweet snacks and desserts. Try to eat less than a teaspoon of salt a day. Too much salt can give you high blood pressure.

Food that is low in salt, sugar, and fat can be delicious! There are many wonderful spices and other ingredients that you can add for flavor. Learn how to cook and eat the healthy way!

1. According to this article, you should D.
   A. eat a lot of salt
   B. eat more protein foods than grains
   C. fry foods
   D. eat fewer desserts

2. C is a protein food.
   A. Butter
   B. Lettuce
   C. Fish
   D. Whole wheat bread

3. Whole grain products DON'T include B.
   A. brown rice
   B. whole milk
   C. whole grain cereal
   D. whole wheat bread

4. Fat from B is unhealthy fat.
   A. fish
   B. mayonnaise
   C. nuts
   D. vegetable oil

5. To prepare lemon chicken, you C.
   A. add two tablespoons of mustard
   B. broil the chicken for forty-five minutes
   C. cut up the chicken before you cook it
   D. microwave it

6. We can infer that chicken skin A.
   A. is fatty
   B. has too much salt
   C. is sweet
   D. is lean

WRITING Your Favorite Healthy Foods

What fruits do you like? What are your favorite vegetables? What are your favorite protein foods? What other healthy foods do you like? Write about them.

PROJECT A Class Recipe Book

Write a recipe for your favorite healthy food. Share your recipe with the class. Then work together and make a class recipe book!

Choose the correct answer.

1. The doctor measured my _A_.
   A. height
   B. heart
   C. health
   D. tests

2. The technician will take _C_.
   A. an examination room
   B. your eyes, ears, nose, and throat
   C. an X-ray
   D. a medical checkup

3. My doctor is concerned about my weight. She put me on a _B_.
   A. physical examination
   B. diet
   C. stethoscope
   D. suggestion

4. My pie wasn't very good. I didn't follow the _D_ in the cookbook.
   A. blueprints
   B. construction
   C. exercises
   D. instructions

5. Do you know any _B_ for a cold?
   A. recipes
   B. remedies
   C. questions
   D. problems

6. My doctor says I must lose some _C_.
   A. energy
   B. advice
   C. weight
   D. blood pressure

7. I always read the label carefully. Many medicines have _A_.
   A. side effects
   B. pharmacies
   C. ailments
   D. ingredients

8. This food is healthy because it has a lot of _D_.
   A. fat
   B. salt
   C. sugar
   D. vitamins

Look at the medicine labels. Choose the correct answer.

Paxton's Pain Medicine
Directions
Adults: Take 2 tablets every 4 hours, or 3 tablets every 6 hours.
Children 6 years to under 12 years: 1 tablet every 6 hours.
Use before 11/15/12

Comfort Cold Medicine
Directions
Adults: Take 2 capsules 4 times a day.
Children 6 years to under 12 years: 1 capsule twice a day.
Use before 9/15/12

Victor's Cough Syrup

Directions:	
Adults & children 12 years of age and over: 4 teaspoons twice a day.	Children 6 years to under 12 years: 2 teaspoons twice a day
Stop use and see a doctor if cough lasts more than 5 days.	

9. Adults can take ____.
   A. 16 teaspoons of Victor's Cough Syrup a day
   B. 8 Comfort Cold capsules a day
   C. 15 Comfort Cold capsules a day
   D. 3 Paxton's Pain tablets every 4 hours

10. Nine-year-old children can take _C_ a day.
    A. 12 Paxton's Pain tablets
    B. 8 teaspoons of Victor's Cough Syrup
    C. 4 Paxton Pain tablets
    D. 4 Comfort Cold capsules

SKILLS CHECK ☑

Words:
- ☐ blood pressure
- ☐ blood test
- ☐ cardiogram
- ☐ checkup
- ☐ chest X-ray
- ☐ doctor
- ☐ ears
- ☐ eyes
- ☐ examination
- ☐ health
- ☐ heart
- ☐ height
- ☐ lab technician
- ☐ measure
- ☐ neck
- ☐ nose
- ☐ nurse
- ☐ scale
- ☐ stethoscope
- ☐ throat
- ☐ weight
- ☐ X-ray technician

I can ask & answer:
- ☐ What's the problem?
- ☐ What's the matter?
- ☐ Should I stop eating *rich desserts*?
- ☐ What should I do?
- ☐ Do you have any advice/suggestions?

I can:
- ☐ follow instructions during a medical checkup
- ☐ make a doctor appointment
- ☐ call in sick
- ☐ report a child's absence from school

I can write about:
- ☐ rules in daily life

12

Future Continuous Tense
Time Expressions

- Describing Future Activities
- Expressing Time and Duration
- Making Plans by Telephone
- Handling Wrong-Number Calls
- Leaving and Taking Phone Messages
- Telephone Directory: White Pages, Government Pages, and Yellow Pages
- Using a Telephone Response System

VOCABULARY PREVIEW

1. bathe the dog
2. clean out the garage
3. exercise
4. iron
5. knit
6. mop the floor
7. pay bills
8. rearrange furniture
9. repaint the kitchen
10. sew
11. borrow
12. return

Will They Be Home This Evening?

(I will)	I'll	be working.
(He will)	He'll	
(She will)	She'll	
(It will)	It'll	
(We will)	We'll	
(You will)	You'll	
(They will)	They'll	

A. Will you be home this evening?

B. Yes, I will. I'll be reading.

1. *Amanda*
ironing

2. *Jack*
sewing

3. *Mr. and Mrs. Kramer*
exercising

4. *Omar*
paying bills

5. *you*
knitting

6. *Harriet*
mopping the floor

7. *you and your wife*
bathing the dog

8. *your parents*
rearranging furniture

9.

Hi, Gloria. This Is Arthur.

Hi, Gloria. This is Arthur.
Can I come over and visit this evening?

No, Arthur.
I'm afraid I won't be home this evening.
I'll be shopping at the supermarket.

Oh. Can I come over and visit
TOMORROW evening?

No, Arthur.
I'm afraid I won't be home tomorrow
evening. I'll be working late at the office.

I see. Can I come over and visit this WEEKEND?

No, Arthur. I'll be visiting my sister
in New York.

Oh. Well, can I come over and visit
next Wednesday?

No, Arthur. I'll be visiting my uncle
in the hospital.

How about sometime next SPRING?

No, Arthur.
I'll be getting married next spring.

Oh!!

Good-bye.

When Can You Come Over?

Complete this conversation and practice with another student.

Hello.

Hi, ________.
This is ________.

Hi, ________. What's up?

I'm having some problems with the homework for tomorrow.

Oh. I'll be glad to help.

Thanks. I can come over at ________ o'clock.
Is that okay?

I'm afraid I won't be home at ________ o'clock.
I'll be ________ing. How about ________ o'clock?

No, I won't be able to come over at ________ o'clock.
I'll be ________ing. How about ________ o'clock?

Fine. I'll see you then.

Will You Be Home Today at About Five O'Clock?

A. Hello, Richard. This is Julie. I want to return the tennis racket I borrowed from you last week. Will you be home today at about five o'clock?

B. Yes, I will. I'll be cooking dinner.

A. Oh. Then I won't come over at five.

B. Why not?

A. I don't want to disturb you. You'll be cooking dinner!

B. Don't worry. You won't disturb me.

A. Okay. See you at five.

A. Hello, ________. This is ________. I want to return the ________ I borrowed from you last week. Will you be home today at about ______ o'clock?

B. Yes, I will. I'll be ____________ing.

A. Oh. Then I won't come over at ______.

B. Why not?

A. I don't want to disturb you. You'll be ____________ing!

B. Don't worry. You won't disturb me.

A. Okay. See you at ______.

1. *videotape*
   repainting the kitchen

2. *hammer*
   cleaning out the garage

3. *football*
   ironing

4.

How to Say It!

Calling People on the Telephone

The person you're calling is there.

A. Hello.
B. Hello. This is *David*. May I please speak to *Carol*?
A. Yes. Hold on a moment.

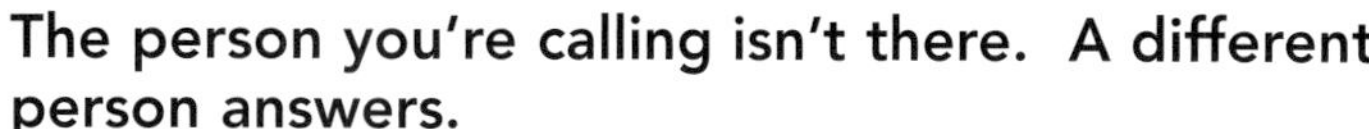

The person you're calling isn't there. A different person answers.

A. Hello.
B. Hello. This is *Maria*. May I please speak to *Kate*?
A. I'm sorry. *Kate* isn't here right now. Can I take a message?
B. Yes. Please tell *Kate* that *Maria* called.
A. Okay.
B. Thank you.

The person you're calling has an answering machine.

A. Hello. This is *Roger*. I'm not here right now. Please leave your name, telephone number, and a brief message after the beep, and I'll call you back. [*beep*]
B. Hi, *Roger*. This is *Eric*. . . .

Practice making telephone calls.

LISTENING

You Have Eight Messages!

Listen to the messages on Bob's machine. Match the messages.

d **1.** Aunt Betty	a. will be repainting the living room.
f **2.** Melanie	b. will be exercising at the health club.
h **3.** Alan	c. will be paying bills.
g **4.** Ms. Wong	d. will be ironing her clothes.
a **5.** Rick and Nancy	e. will be visiting Russia.
c **6.** Denise	f. will be studying for a big test.
e **7.** Dr. Garcia	g. will be working until 8 P.M.
b **8.** Mom and Dad	h. will be attending a wedding.

READING

GROWING UP

Jessica is growing up. Very soon she'll be walking, she'll be talking, and she'll be playing with the other children in the neighborhood. Jessica can't believe how quickly time flies! She won't be a baby very much longer. Soon she'll be a little girl.

Tommy is growing up. Very soon he'll be shaving, he'll be driving, and he'll be going out on dates. Tommy can't believe how quickly time flies! He won't be a little boy very much longer. Soon he'll be a teenager.

Kathy is growing up. Very soon she'll be going to college, she'll be living away from home, and she'll be starting a career. Kathy can't believe how quickly time flies! She won't be a teenager very much longer. Soon she'll be a young adult.

Peter and Sally are getting older. Very soon they'll be getting married, they'll be having children, and they'll be buying a house. Peter and Sally can't believe how quickly time flies! They won't be young adults very much longer. Soon they'll be middle-aged.

Walter is getting older. Very soon he'll be reaching the age of sixty-five, he'll be retiring, and he'll be taking it easy for the first time in his life. Walter can't believe how quickly time flies! He won't be middle-aged very much longer. Soon he'll be a senior citizen.

✔ READING *CHECK-UP*

TRUE OR FALSE?

1. Jessica will be talking soon.
2. Kathy doesn't go to college.
3. Peter and Sally are married.
4. Walter will stop working soon.
5. Tommy is a teenager.
6. Jessica won't be going out on dates very soon.

How About You?
What do you think you'll be doing ten years from now? Tell about your future.

She'll Be Staying with Us for a Few Months

A. How long will your Aunt Gertrude be staying with us?

B. She'll be staying with us **for a few months**.

1. How long will they be staying in Vancouver?
until Friday

2. How much longer will you be working on my car?
for a few more hours

3. How late will your son be studying this evening?
until 8 o'clock

4. How much longer will you be practicing the trombone?
for a few more minutes

5. When will we be arriving in Sydney?
at 7 A.M.

6. How far will we be driving today?
until we reach Milwaukee

7. How much longer will you be chatting online with your friends?
for ten more minutes

8. How soon will Santa Claus be coming?
in a few days

READING

HAPPY THANKSGIVING!

Thanksgiving is this week, and several of our relatives from out of town will be staying with us during the long holiday weekend. Uncle Frank will be staying for a few days. He'll be sleeping in the room over the garage. Grandma and Grandpa will be staying until next Monday. They'll be sleeping in the master bedroom. Cousin Ben will be staying until Saturday. He'll be sleeping in the guest room. Cousin Bertha will be staying for a week. She'll be sleeping on a cot in the children's bedroom. (My wife and I will be sleeping downstairs on the convertible sofa in the living room.)

Our family will be busy for the next few days. My wife and I will be preparing Thanksgiving dinner, and our children will be cleaning the house from top to bottom. We're looking forward to the holiday, but we know we'll be happy when it's over.

Happy Thanksgiving!

✓ READING *CHECK-UP*

Q & A

Uncle Frank, Grandma, Grandpa, Cousin Ben, and Cousin Bertha are calling to ask about the plans for Thanksgiving. Using this model, create dialogs based on the story.

A. Hi! This is *Uncle Frank*!
B. Hi, *Uncle Frank*! How are you?
A. Fine!
B. We're looking forward to seeing you for Thanksgiving.
A. Actually, that's why I'm calling. Are you sure there will be enough room for me?
B. Don't worry! We'll have plenty of room. You'll be sleeping *in the room over the garage*. Will that be okay?
A. That'll be fine.
B. By the way, *Uncle Frank*, how long will you be staying with us?
A. *For a few days.*
B. That's great! We're really looking forward to seeing you.

PRONUNCIATION Contractions with *Will*

Listen. Then say it.	**Say it. Then listen.**
Yes, I will. I'll be cooking.	Yes, I will. I'll be cleaning.
Yes, he will. He'll be baking.	Yes, she will. She'll be studying.
Yes, it will. It'll be raining.	Yes, you will. You'll be working.
Yes, we will. We'll be reading.	Yes, they will. They'll be sleeping.

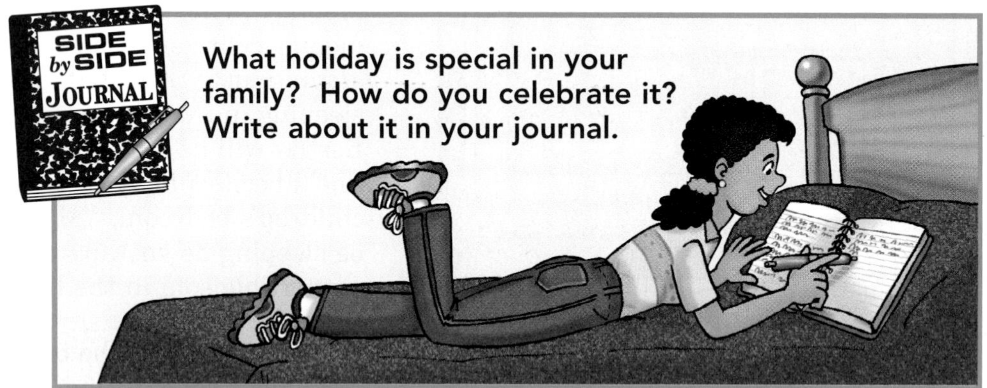

What holiday is special in your family? How do you celebrate it? Write about it in your journal.

GRAMMAR FOCUS

FUTURE CONTINUOUS TENSE

(I will)	I'll	be working.
(He will)	He'll	
(She will)	She'll	
(It will)	It'll	
(We will)	We'll	
(You will)	You'll	
(They will)	They'll	

TIME EXPRESSIONS

I'll be staying	for	a few months.
		a few more hours.
		a few more minutes.
	until	Friday.
		10 o'clock.
		we reach Milwaukee.

We'll be arriving	at 7 A.M.
	in a few days.

Complete the sentences with the future continuous tense and *for, until,* or *at*.

1. A. How long _____ your parents _____ staying in Montreal?
   B. _____ staying there _____ a week.
2. A. How late _____ you and your wife _____ cleaning your garage?
   B. _____ cleaning it _____ six o'clock.
3. A. When _____ Uncle George _____ arriving?
   B. _____ arriving _____ 10:45 this morning.
4. A. _____ you be home tonight?
   B. Yes, _____. _____ reading _____ I get tired.
5. A. When _____ the train _____ leaving?
   B. _____ leaving _____ exactly 9:19.
6. A. How much longer _____ your daughter _____ practicing the piano?
   B. _____ practicing _____ ten more minutes.

LIFE SKILLS

• Telephone conversations • Taking phone messages

1 CONVERSATION Wrong Numbers

Practice conversations with your classmates. Dial a wrong number!

A. Hello.
B. Hello. Is this ___(name)___?
A. I'm sorry. There's nobody here named ___(name)___.
B. Is this ___(phone number)___?
A. No, it isn't.
B. I apologize. I dialed the wrong number.

2 CONVERSATION Leaving a Message

Practice the conversation with a classmate.

Carla—
David called
417-624-9358

A. Hello.
B. Hello. This is David. May I speak with Carla?
A. Just a moment. Let me see if she's here.
B. Thanks.

. . .

A. Sorry. She isn't here right now. Can I take a message?
B. Yes. Please tell her that David called. My telephone number is 417-624-9358.
A. Okay.
B. Thank you.

3 CONVERSATION & WRITING Taking Phone Messages

Practice with a classmate. Write down the messages.

A. Hello.
B. Hello. This is ______. May I speak with ______?
A. Just a moment. Let me see if he's/she's here.
B. Thanks.

. . .

A. Sorry. He/She isn't here right now. Can I take a message?
B. Yes. Please tell him/her that ______ called. My telephone number is ______.
A. Okay.
B. Thank you.

1.

2.

3.

TAFT Diane 472 Maple Lit	252 478-3296
Jane & Mark 15 Hill Con	252 853-9701
M A 86 Walnut Lit	252 478-5783
Peter 174 Rogers Bri	252 876-0021
TAGGART Robert D 19 Davis Bra	336 793-0065
Robert P 1655 E Pine Con	252 853-7428
Tammie 425 College Cop	336 516-6735
TAI Lan 262 Birch Lin	336 392-6163
TALBOT Beth 243 Mill Bri	252 876-5218
Mark 32 Green Cop	336 793-2804
Vera & George 222 Congress Bri	252 478-6635
TALIENTO A & S 466 Ridge Lin	336 392-1306
Carlo 94 Laurel Lin	336 392-2854

BRANDON TOWN OF

AMBULANCE/FIRE & RESCUE	
EMERGENCY CALLS ONLY	911
For All Other Business	336 793-3670
Animal Control Office	336 638-8621
Board of Health	336 638-3792
Building Inspector	336 793-4611
Highway Department	336 793-5900
Library 253 Park Bran	336 638-8156
Parks & Recreation	336 638-6258
POLICE —	
EMERGENCY CALLS ONLY	911
For All Other Business	336 793-4500
Recycling	336 638-5415
SCHOOLS —	
King Elementary School	336 634-1200
Lincoln Middle School	336 634-1400
Brandon High School	336 634-1600

Circle the answers on the telephone directory page above.

1. What is Lan Tai's phone number?
2. What is Carlo Taliento's address?
3. What is Robert Paul Taggart's phone number?
4. What is Mark Talbot's phone number?
5. What is Mary Ann Taft's address?
6. What is Armando and Sandra Taliento's telephone number?
7. What is George Talbot's address?

Choose the correct answer.

8. Jane and Mark Taft live in ___.
   A. Conway C. Copeland
   B. Brandon D. Littleton

9. Robert Daniel Taggart lives in ___.
   A. Conway C. Copeland
   B. Brandon D. Bridgeton

10. The area code for ___ is 252.
   A. Copeland C. Littleton
   B. Brandon D. Linwood

11. The phone number for ___ is on a different directory page.
   A. Amy Tan C. Arthur Tenny
   B. Rose Tallman D. Lisa Tate

12. Call ___ if someone is having a heart attack.
   A. 336 793-3670 C. 336 793-4500
   B. 911 D. 336 638-3792

13. Call ___ if there's a dangerous dog in the neighborhood.
   A. 336 638-3792 C. 336 793-5900
   B. 336 793-3670 D. 336 638-8621

14. Call ___ if someone just stole your wallet.
   A. 336 793-3670 C. 336 793-4500
   B. 336 638-3792 D. 911

15. Call ___ to ask about free flu shots.
   A. 336 793-4500 C. 336 638-5415
   B. 336 638-3792 D. 336 638-8156

16. Call ___ if a traffic light isn't working.
   A. 336 793-5900 C. 336 638-6258
   B. 336 793-3670 D. 911

17. Call ___ if your landlord won't repair the stairs in your building.
   A. 336 793-4500 C. 336 793-4611
   B. 336 638-3792 D. 336 793-3670

18. Call ___ if you have an old refrigerator you don't need anymore.
   A. 336 638-3792 C. 336 638-5415
   B. 336 793-4611 D. 336 793-3670

19. Call ___ to register your 5-year-old daughter for kindergarten next year.
   A. 336 634-1200 C. 336 634-1600
   B. 336 634-1400 D. 336 638-8156

LIFE SKILLS READING

- Yellow Pages
- Using a telephone response system

YELLOW PAGES

HOSPITALS

King Medical Center
250 Central Mul 765 269–1580

Mount Hope Hospital
586 Riverway Mid
General Information 812 379–4200
Emergency Department 812 379–4300
Clinic 812 379–3054
Pharmacy 812 379–4703

HOTELS & MOTELS

BROOKSIDE HOTEL *—see our ad this page*
93 South Med 765 516–6702

Hillside Motel
15 Waterview Mul 765 246–3065

Oakwood Hotel
772 Brighton Mil 765 921–5724

VILLAGE GREEN HOTEL *—see our ad this page*
715 Raymond Mit 812 489–8831

WHITE PINES INN *—see our ad this page*
212 Grove Mul 765 269–7050

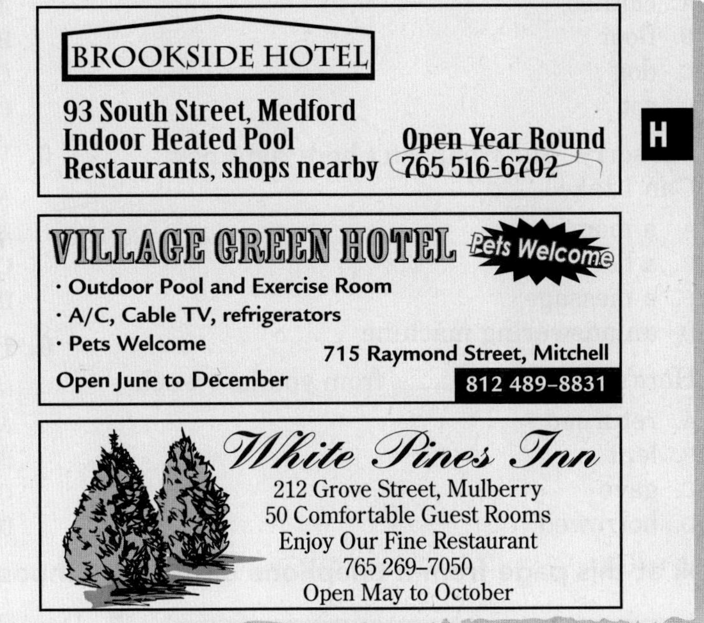

BROOKSIDE HOTEL
93 South Street, Medford
Indoor Heated Pool
Restaurants, shops nearby
Open Year Round
765 516-6702
VILLAGE GREEN HOTEL
Pets Welcome
· Outdoor Pool and Exercise Room
· A/C, Cable TV, refrigerators
· Pets Welcome
715 Raymond Street, Mitchell
Open June to December
812 489-8831
White Pines Inn
212 Grove Street, Mulberry
50 Comfortable Guest Rooms
Enjoy Our Fine Restaurant
765 269–7050
Open May to October

H

Circle the following information in the telephone directory listings above.

1. The address of a hospital in Mulberry.
2. The phone number of a hotel in Milton.
3. The address of a hotel with an outdoor pool.
4. The phone number of a hotel with a restaurant.
5. The phone number of a clinic in Midland.
6. The address of a hotel that is open in April.
7. The phone number of a hospital pharmacy.
8. The phone number of a hotel where you can bring your dog.

A TELEPHONE RESPONSE SYSTEM

When you call the Save-Mart store, an automated response system answers. Follow the instructions and answer the questions.

Thank you for calling Save-Mart Department Store.

- For gift card information, press 1.
- To locate a Save-Mart near you, press 2.
- To place an order, press 3.
- To check the delivery date of an order, press 4.
- If you are calling with a question about your credit card account, press 5.
- To add your name to our mailing list, press 6.
- For customer service, press 7.

1. Jeffrey wants to talk to a customer service representative. He should press ____.
   A. 2 B. 3 C. 6 D. 7
2. Susan thinks there's a mistake on her credit card bill. She should press ____.
   A. 1 B. 4 C. 5 D. 6
3. Monica wants to know the day her TV is going to arrive. She should press ____.
   A. 2 B. 3 C. 4 D. 6
4. Bruno is looking for the nearest Save-Mart store. He should press ____.
   A. 2 B. 3 C. 6 D. 7
5. Edna wants to order a computer. She should press ____.
   A. 1 B. 3 C. 4 D. 5

ASSESSMENT • Check-up test • Self-evaluation checklists

Choose the correct answer.

1. I'll be mopping the ___ this evening.
   - A. clothes
   - B. floor
   - C. dog
   - D. cot
2. I'm sorry. Ms. Wong isn't here right now. Can I take ___?
   - A. a moment
   - B. a beep
   - C. a message
   - D. an answering machine
3. Here's the plate I ___ from you last week.
   - A. returned
   - B. lent
   - C. gave
   - D. borrowed
4. We'll be ___ in Chicago until Sunday.
   - A. staying
   - B. arriving
   - C. looking forward
   - D. disturbing
5. William is middle-aged. Soon he'll be a ___.
   - A. young adult
   - B. teenager
   - C. senior citizen
   - D. little boy
6. I'll be busy on Saturday. I'll be attending ___.
   - A. bills
   - B. the garage
   - C. furniture
   - D. a wedding

Look at this page from a telephone directory. Choose the correct answer.

183 SANBORN—SATO		
SANBORN Erica	917 Main Gre	573 544-2975
T R	43 Pine Gle	314 232-7736
SANCHEZ D & N	16 High Can	573 675-8920
David N	573 Broadway Map	314 899-4467
P & M	425 First Cla	314 337-2927
SANDLER D M	75 Maple Can	573 675-0098
D & N	32 Green Cla	314 337-2278
Norman	32 Green Mal	573 454-4187
SANDS Louisa	357 Willow Gre	573 544-1989
Robert L	223 Grove Cla	314 337-3378
SANTANA L	468 King Mal	573 454-4212
R & L	773 West Map	314 899-4926
SANTOS Ramon	115 Kent Gle	314 232-7721

7. Daniel and Norma Sandler live in ___.
   - A. Glendale
   - B. Canton
   - C. Clayton
   - D. Greenville
8. The phone number for Rosa and Luis Santana is ___.
   - A. 314-337-3378
   - B. 314-899-4926
   - C. 573-454-4212
   - D. 573-544-1989
9. The area code for ___ is 314.
   - A. Greenville
   - B. Malden
   - C. Glendale
   - D. Canton
10. The phone number for ___ is on a different directory page.
    - A. Marian Saunders
    - B. J. P. Sarrouf
    - C. Angela Sarmiento
    - D. Kenji Sasaki

SKILLS CHECK ☑

Words:

- ☐ bathe
- ☐ borrow
- ☐ clean out
- ☐ come over
- ☐ disturb
- ☐ exercise
- ☐ grow up
- ☐ iron
- ☐ knit
- ☐ mop
- ☐ pay bills
- ☐ rearrange
- ☐ repaint
- ☐ retire
- ☐ return
- ☐ sew
- ☐ message
- ☐ telephone directory
- ☐ wrong number
- ☐ ambulance
- ☐ animal control office
- ☐ board of health
- ☐ building inspector
- ☐ fire & rescue
- ☐ highway department
- ☐ library
- ☐ parks & recreation
- ☐ police
- ☐ recycling
- ☐ schools

I can ask & answer:

- ☐ Will *you* be home *this evening*?
  Yes, *I* will. *I'll* be *reading*.
- ☐ Will you be home today at about *five o'clock*?
- ☐ Can I come over and visit *this evening*?
- ☐ How long/How much longer/How late will *you* be *studying*?
- ☐ When/How soon will *we* be *arriving*?
- ☐ How far will *we* be *driving*?

I can write about:

- ☐ how my family celebrates a holiday

I can leave and take telephone messages:

- ☐ Hello. This is *David*. May I (please) speak to/with *Carol*?
  Just a moment. Let me see if *she's* here.
  Yes. Hold on a moment.
  Sorry./I'm sorry. *Carol* isn't here right now. Can I take a message?
  Please tell *Carol* that *David* called.

I can:

- ☐ use the white pages, yellow pages, and government pages in the telephone directory
- ☐ use an automated telephone response system

Some/Any
Pronoun Review
Verb Tense Review

- Offering Help
- Indicating Ownership
- Household Problems
- Requesting Maintenance and Repairs
- Reading a Rental Agreement
- Tenants' Rights
- Friends

Vocabulary Preview

1. electrician
2. locksmith
3. mechanic
4. plumber
5. repairperson
6. downstairs neighbor
7. upstairs neighbor
8. next-door neighbor
9. dishwasher
10. faucet
11. garbage disposal
12. lock
13. video camera/camcorder

I'll Be Glad to Help

I	me	my	mine	myself
you	you	your	yours	yourself
he	him	his	his	himself
she	her	her	hers	herself
it	it	its	—	itself
we	us	our	ours	ourselves
you	you	your	yours	yourselves
they	them	their	theirs	themselves

A. What's **Johnny** doing?

B. **He's** getting dressed.

A. Does **he** need any help?
I'll be glad to help **him**.

B. No, that's okay. **He** can get dressed by **himself**.

1. *your daughter*
feed the canary

2. *your husband*
clean the garage

3. *your children*
make lunch

4. *you*
do my homework

5. *your sister*
wash her car

6. *Jim and Nancy*
rake the leaves

7. *Tom*
paint the fence

8. *you and your husband*
bathe the dog

9.

I Just Found This Watch

A. I just found this watch. Is it yours?

B. No, it isn't mine. But it might be **Fred's**. **He** lost **his** a few days ago.

A. Really? I'll call **him** right away.

B. When you talk to **him**, tell **him** I said "Hello."

1. *umbrella*

2. *wallet*

3. *notebook*

4. *camera*

5. *calculator*

6. *headphones*

7. *ring*

8. *sunglasses*

9. *cell phone*

10. *address book*

11. *briefcase*

12.

I Couldn't Fall Asleep Last Night

A. You look tired today.

B. Yes, I know. I couldn't fall asleep last night.

A. Why not?

B. My **neighbors** were **arguing**.

A. How late did they **argue**?

B. Believe it or not, they **argued** until 3 A.M.!

A. That's terrible! Did you call and complain?

B. No, I didn't. I don't like to complain.

A. Well, I hope you sleep better tonight.

B. I'm sure I will. My **neighbors** don't **argue** very often.

1. *downstairs neighbor*
   sing

2. *neighbor's* dog*
   bark

3. *upstairs neighbors*
   vacuum their apartment

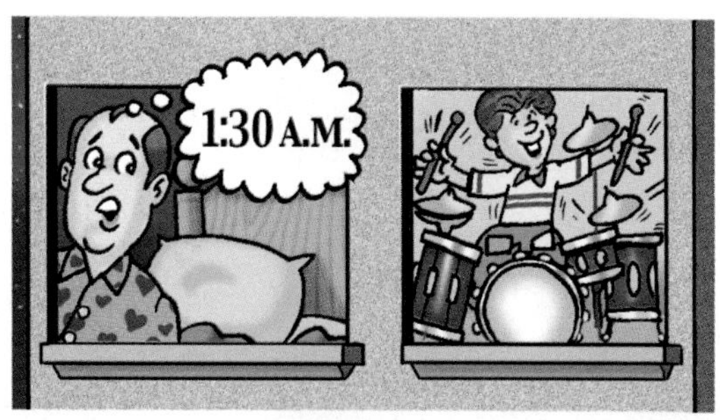

4. *neighbors'* son*
   play the drums

* neighbor – neighbor's dog
neighbors – neighbors' son

5. *neighbor across the hall*
   dance

6. *neighbors' daughter*
   listen to loud music

7. *next-door neighbors*
   rearrange their furniture

8. *neighbor's cat*
   cry

9. *neighbors' son*
   lift weights

10.

ON YOUR OWN *Neighbors*

Do you know your neighbors? Are they friendly? Are they helpful?
Do you sometimes have problems with your neighbors?

Talk with other students about your neighbors.

Do You Know Anybody Who Can Help Me?

something	anything
somebody / someone	anybody / anyone

A. There's something wrong with my **washing machine**.

B. I'm sorry. I can't help you. I don't know ANYTHING about **washing machines**.

A. Do you know anybody who can help me?

B. Not really. You should look in the phone book. I'm sure you'll find somebody who can fix it.

1. *refrigerator*

2. *dishwasher*

3. *kitchen faucet*

4. *garbage disposal*

5. *computer*

6. *bathtub*

7. *video camera*

8.

Can You Send a Plumber?

A. Armstrong Plumbing Company. Can I help you?

B. Yes. There's something wrong with my kitchen sink. Can you send a plumber to fix it as soon as possible?

A. Where do you live?

B. 156 Grove Street in Centerville.

A. I can send a plumber tomorrow morning. Is that okay?

B. Not really. I'm afraid I won't be home tomorrow morning. I'll be taking my son to the dentist.

A. How about tomorrow afternoon?

B. Tomorrow afternoon? What time?

A. Between one and four.

B. That's fine. Somebody will be here then.

A. What's the name?

B. Helen Bradley.

A. And what's the address again?

B. 156 Grove Street in Centerville.

A. And the phone number?

B. 237-9180.

A. Okay. We'll have someone there tomorrow afternoon.

B. Thank you.

A. ____________________. Can I help you?

B. Yes. There's something wrong with my __________.
Can you send a __________ to fix it as soon as possible?

A. Where do you live?

B. ______________ in ______________.

A. I can send a __________ tomorrow morning. Is that okay?

B. Not really. I'm afraid I won't be home tomorrow morning.
I'll be ______________ing.

A. How about tomorrow afternoon?

B. Tomorrow afternoon? What time?

A. Between ______ and ______.

B. That's fine. Somebody will be here then.

A. What's the name?

B. ____________________.

A. And what's the address again?

B. ______________ in ______________.

A. And the phone number?

B. __________.

A. Okay. We'll have someone there tomorrow afternoon.

B. Thank you.

1. *Ajax Home Electronics Service*
repairperson

2. *Ace Electrical Repair*
electrician

3. *Patty's Plumbing and Heating*
plumber

4. *Larry's Lock Repair*
locksmith

TROUBLE WITH CARS

It might seem hard to believe, but my friends and I are all having trouble with our cars. There's something wrong with all of them!

Charlie is having trouble with his. The brakes don't work. He tried to fix them by himself, but he wasn't able to, since he doesn't know anything about cars. Finally, he took the car to his mechanic. The mechanic charged him a lot of money, and the brakes STILL don't work! Charlie is really annoyed. He's having a lot of trouble with his car, and he can't find anybody who can help him.

Betty is having trouble with hers. It doesn't start in the morning. She tried to fix it by herself, but she wasn't able to, since she doesn't know anything about cars. Finally, she took the car to her mechanic. The mechanic charged her a lot of money, and the car STILL doesn't start in the morning! Betty is really annoyed. She's having a lot of trouble with her car, and she can't find anybody who can help her.

Mark and Nancy are having trouble with theirs. The steering wheel doesn't turn. They tried to fix it by themselves, but they weren't able to, since they don't know anything about cars. Finally, they took the car to their mechanic. The mechanic charged them a lot of money, and the steering wheel STILL doesn't turn! Mark and Nancy are really annoyed. They're having a lot of trouble with their car, and they can't find anybody who can help them.

I'm having trouble with mine, too. The windows don't go up and down. I tried to fix them by myself, but I wasn't able to, since I don't know anything about cars. Finally, I took the car to my mechanic. The mechanic charged me a lot of money, and the windows STILL don't go up and down! I'm really annoyed. I'm having a lot of trouble with my car, and I can't find anybody who can help me.

✓ READING *CHECK-UP*

WHAT'S THE WORD?

1. Charlie tried to fix _______ car by _______.
2. Mark and Nancy's mechanic charged _______ a lot and still didn't fix _______ car.
3. Betty can't find anybody to help _______ fix _______ car.
4. I'm having trouble with _______ car, too. _______ starts in the morning, but the windows are broken.
5. The windows don't go up and down. I tried to fix _______ by _______, but I couldn't.
6. My friends and I can't fix _______ cars by _______, and we're all very angry at _______ mechanics.

LISTENING

WHAT'S THE WORD?

Listen and choose the word you hear.

1.	a. him	b. her
2.	a. him	b. them
3.	a. them	b. him
4.	a. yours	b. hers
5.	a. yourself	b. yourselves
6.	a. our	b. her

WHAT ARE THEY TALKING ABOUT?

Listen and choose what the people are talking about.

1.	a. stove	b. sink
2.	a. dishwasher	b. garbage disposal
3.	a. TV	b. camcorder
4.	a. headphones	b. cell phone
5.	a. windows	b. car

Are you "handy"? Do you like to fix things? Tell about something you fixed. What was the problem? How did you fix it? Also, tell about something you COULDN'T fix. What was the problem? What did you do?

How to Say It!

Giving Advice

A. I'm having trouble with my *car*.

B. { You should / You ought to / I think you should / I think you ought to } *take it to a mechanic.*

Practice conversations with other students. Talk about problems and give advice.

IN YOUR OWN WORDS

For Writing and Discussion

THAT'S WHAT FRIENDS ARE FOR!

Frank has some very nice friends. He sees his friends often. When he needs help, they're always happy to help him. For example, last week Frank moved to a new apartment. He couldn't move everything by himself, and he didn't really have enough money to hire a moving company. His friends came over and helped him move everything. He was very grateful. His friends said, "We're happy to help you, Frank. That's what friends are for!"

Emma has some very special friends. She sees her friends often. When she needs help, they're always happy to help her. For example, last month the faucet broke in Emma's kitchen and flooded her apartment. There was water in every room. She couldn't fix everything herself, and her superintendent didn't help her at all. Her friends came over and helped her fix the faucet and clean up every room in the apartment. She was very grateful. Her friends said, "We're happy to help you, Emma. That's what friends are for!"

It's nice to have friends you can rely on when you need help. Tell about a time when your friends helped you. Tell about a time when you helped a friend.

PRONUNCIATION Deleted *h*

Listen. Then say it.

Tell him I said "Hello."

I'll be glad to help him.

He can get dressed by himself.

The mechanic charged him a lot of money.

Say it. Then listen.

Tell her I said "Hello."

I'll be glad to help her.

She can make lunch by herself.

The mechanic charged her a lot of money.

Think about a very good friend. Write about this person in your journal.

GRAMMAR FOCUS

Pronoun Review

Subject Pronouns	Object Pronouns	Possessive Adjectives	Possessive Pronouns	Reflexive Pronouns
I	me	my	mine	myself
you	you	your	yours	yourself
he	him	his	his	himself
she	her	her	hers	herself
it	it	its	—	itself
we	us	our	ours	ourselves
you	you	your	yours	yourselves
they	them	their	theirs	themselves

Some/Any

There's **something** wrong with my washing machine.
I'm sure you'll find **somebody/someone** who can fix it.
I don't know **anything** about washing machines.
Do you know **anybody/anyone** who can help me?

Possessive of Singular & Plural Nouns

neighbor – neighbor's dog
neighbors – neighbors' son

Complete the sentences.

1. A. Does your son need any help? I'll be glad to help ______.
   B. No. That's okay. ______ can fix ______ bicycle by ______.
2. A. Is this newspaper ______ or Mr. and Mrs. Lee's?
   B. It isn't mine. I think it's ______.
3. A. Does your daughter need any help? I'll be glad to help ______.
   B. No. That's okay. ______ can do ______ homework by ______.
4. A. How did ______ hurt yourself?
   B. I hurt ______ while I was moving ______ piano.
5. A. How often do you speak to ______ grandparents?
   B. I call ______ every Sunday, and ______ call me every Wednesday.
6. A. Did your parents enjoy ______ at the concert last night?
   B. Yes, ______ did. You should get a ticket for tonight's concert. I'm sure ______ and your wife will enjoy ______.
7. A. Whose cell phone is this? Is ______ yours, your son's, or your wife's?
   B. It isn't ______. My cell phone is larger. It isn't ______ son's. ______ is smaller. It isn't ______ wife's. ______ is newer.
8. A. You look upset. What's the matter?
   B. We're having a problem. There's something wrong with ______ front door. ______ doesn't open. Do you know anybody who can help ______? ______ can't fix our front door by ______.

LIFE SKILLS

• Requesting maintenance & repairs in a rental unit

1 CONVERSATION Following Up on a Request for Maintenance

You called a few days ago to request a repair in your apartment, but nobody fixed it. Call again! Practice conversations with your classmates.

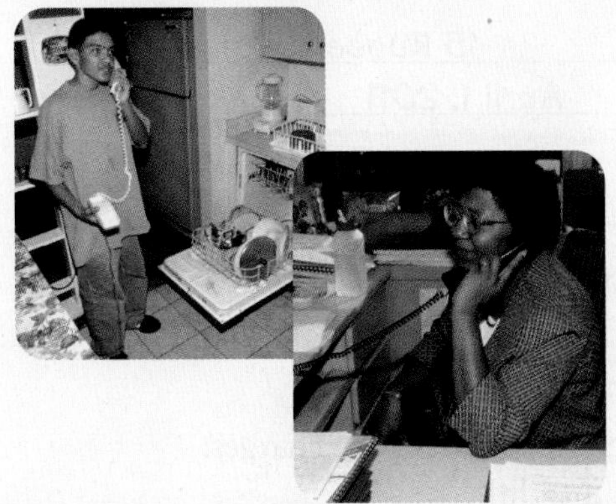

A. Hello. This is ____________ in apartment ____.

B. Yes. How can I help you?

A. I called a few days ago. My ____________ is broken.

B. I'm sorry. Please tell me the problem again.

A. ______________________________

B. Okay. I'll make sure someone checks your ____________ today.

A. Thank you very much.

1. dishwasher
It's leaking.

2. stove
Two burners don't light.

3. lock
The key gets stuck.

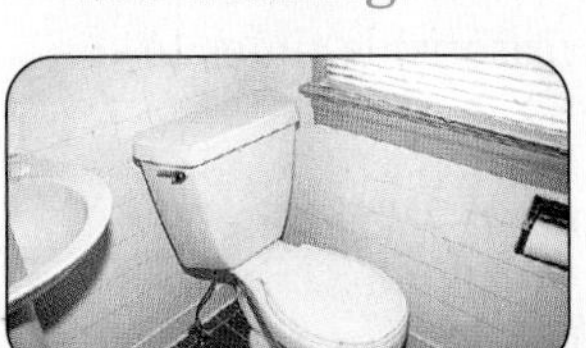

4. toilet
The water keeps running, and the toilet doesn't flush properly.

5. kitchen sink
The water drips, and the drain is clogged.

6. heat
The apartment doesn't get warm.

THINK, SHARE, & SOLVE What are other common maintenance and repair problems in a rental unit? What should a tenant do if the building manager doesn't fix a problem? Discuss as a class.

2 WRITING A Repair Request Form

You have a problem in your apartment! Fill out the form to request a repair.

APARTMENT MAINTENANCE/REPAIR REQUEST FORM

NAME: ______________________________

ADDRESS: ______________________________

PROBLEM/WORK REQUIRED: ______________________________

____

Is there a pet in the residence? ___ Yes ___ No
(If Yes, the pet must be secured or the maintenance person will not enter the residence.)

Do you give permission to the maintenance person to enter the residence if you are not at home? ___ Yes ___ No

______________ Tenant's Signature ___/___/___ Date ________ Time AM PM (circle)

Read the rental agreement and answer the questions.

Rental Agreement

This agreement is between: Lenora Garcia as LANDLORD and Frank P. Warner as TENANT.

The LANDLORD leases to the TENANT apartment number 7 at 15 Russell Street Bryan, Texas 77802 for the term of twelve months beginning April 1, 2011 and ending on March 31, 2012.

TERMS AND CONDITIONS OF THIS AGREEMENT:

1. **RENT:** The total rent for the apartment is $10,500.00. The monthly rent is $875.00 due on or before the first day of each month. If the TENANT does not pay the rent before the fifteenth of the month, the LANDLORD will charge a late fee of 4% of the monthly rent.
2. **UTILITIES AND SERVICES:** The TENANT will pay the following utility and service charges: Gas, Electricity, Cable TV, Telephone, and Internet.
3. **APPLIANCES:** The apartment is rented with the following appliances: Refrigerator and Stove. The LANDLORD will repair appliances that the LANDLORD owns that need repair due to normal use. The TENANT is responsible for repairing any other appliances.
4. **SECURITY DEPOSIT:** The TENANT will deposit with the LANDLORD a security deposit of $875.00. If the apartment is in good condition when the TENANT moves out, and all rent is paid, the LANDLORD will return the full amount of the security deposit within 30 days.
5. **ENTRY TO APARTMENT:** The LANDLORD has the right to enter the apartment at reasonable times to inspect the apartment or to make repairs if the LANDLORD gives 24-hour notice.
6. **CONDITION OF APARTMENT:** The TENANT agrees to take good care of the apartment. When the agreement ends, the TENANT will return the apartment in good clean condition.
7. **NOISE:** The LANDLORD can end this agreement if other tenants in the building complain about any loud noises (i.e. parties, music, etc.).

1. _____ $875 every month.
- A. The security deposit is
- B. The late fee is
- C. The rent is
- D. The utilities are

2. The rental agreement is for _____.
- A. one month
- B. two months
- C. the month of April
- D. one year

3. Frank Warner can move into the apartment on _____.
- A. April 1, 2011
- B. March 31, 2011
- C. March 31, 2012
- D. April 1, 2012

4. The tenant does NOT have to pay the _____.
- A. gas bill
- B. telephone bill
- C. water bill
- D. electric bill

5. The tenant has to _____.
- A. enter the apartment at reasonable times
- B. repair the stove if it doesn't work
- C. complain about loud noises
- D. pay a 4% late fee if the rent is 15 days late

6. According to the agreement, the landlord CANNOT enter the tenant's apartment _____.
- A. to fix things
- B. if he doesn't tell the tenant the day before
- C. when the tenant isn't there
- D. to check the condition of the apartment

Read this tenants' rights notice and answer the questions.

KNOW YOUR RIGHTS! Advice for tenants from the Franklin County Fair Housing Council

As a tenant, it's important to know your rights. According to state law, tenants have the right to an apartment that is safe and healthy to live in. The heating, plumbing, and electricity must work. The windows, doors, walls, roof, floors, and stairways must be in good condition. The building and the land around it must be clean. The apartment must have a bathroom with a toilet, sink, and bathtub or shower, and a kitchen with a sink. All of these must be in working condition. The apartment must also have windows that open in each room, safe fire or emergency exits, smoke detectors that work, and locks on outside doors and windows.

With these tenant rights, there are also responsibilities—things that you, as a tenant, have to do. You must take good care of your apartment, follow all the rules in your rental agreement or lease, and tell the landlord promptly when there are problems that need repairs. If you do all these things, your landlord has to fix problems that make the apartment unsafe and unhealthy to live in.

If your landlord won't make important repairs, call your city's code enforcement office or health department. You also have the right to pay for the repair and deduct the cost from your rent. For example, if it costs $300 to repair the sink and your rent is $800, you pay the landlord only $500.

Tenants often have questions about security deposits. How much can a landlord charge, and how long can he or she keep the money? According to state law, the security deposit for most apartments can't be more than twice the monthly rent. When the tenant moves out, the landlord must return the security deposit within 21 days if the apartment is in good condition. The landlord can use some or all of the security deposit to clean or repair the apartment, but only if the tenant caused the problem. The landlord has to return any money that he or she doesn't use for cleaning or repairs. If your landlord doesn't return your security deposit or keeps more than you think is right, you can talk to a lawyer and take your landlord to court.

A landlord cannot evict you from your apartment because you complained to your city's code enforcement office, made a repair and deducted it from your rent, or went to court about a housing problem. A landlord can never turn off your heat or electricity or put your things on the street. If a landlord changes the locks on your door, the landlord must give you the new key.

1. A tenant does NOT have to ____.
- A. take good care of the apartment
- B. fix problems that make the apartment unsafe
- C. follow the rules in the lease
- D. tell the landlord when the smoke detectors don't work

2. Call your city's health department if your landlord ____.
- A. won't return your security deposit
- B. changes the locks on your door
- C. complains
- D. won't fix a broken toilet

3. An apartment in Franklin County does NOT have to have ____.
- A. a kitchen with a sink
- B. windows that open
- C. a bathtub and a shower
- D. locks on outside doors

4. If you pay $900 a month rent in Franklin County, your security deposit can't be more than ____.
- A. $900
- B. $1,000
- C. $1,600
- D. $1,800

5. A landlord CANNOT ____.
- A. turn off a tenant's heat and electricity
- B. use a security deposit for repairs
- C. use a security deposit for cleaning
- D. return a security deposit twenty days after a tenant moves out

6. When a family deducts $100 from their $700 rent because they paid for a repair, they pay the landlord ____.
- A. $100
- B. $600
- C. $700
- D. $800

SHARE & COMPARE Do you have a lease or rental agreement? Bring it to class and compare with other students. What tenants' rights and responsibilities are in the agreements? Discuss as a class.

Choose the correct answer.

1. My upstairs neighbors were rearranging _____ until late at night.
   A. their faucet
   B. loud music
   C. their furniture
   D. the downstairs neighbors

2. If you look in the _____, you'll find somebody who can fix your sink.
   A. phone
   B. phone book
   C. plumber
   D. plumbing company

3. We were upset. The electrician _____ us a lot of money to fix our light.
   A. charged
   B. changed
   C. gave
   D. showed

4. When I move to my new apartment, I'm going to _____ a moving company.
   A. buy
   B. retire
   C. fire
   D. hire

5. We'll be busy all morning. We'll be raking _____.
   A. cookies
   B. lunch
   C. leaves
   D. the dog

6. I'm having a problem with my _____. Sometimes it doesn't start.
   A. apartment
   B. car
   C. key
   D. living room window

7. We have to pay our _____ on or before the first day of each month.
   A. rental agreement
   B. lease
   C. security deposit
   D. rent

8. The landlord has to fix any _____ that needs repair.
   A. tenant
   B. gas
   C. appliance
   D. agreement

9. I'm going to _____ the cost of the repair from my rent.
   A. evict
   B. deduct
   C. return
   D. change

10. According to the law, every tenant has the _____ to a safe apartment.
    A. right
    B. rule
    C. responsibility
    D. condition

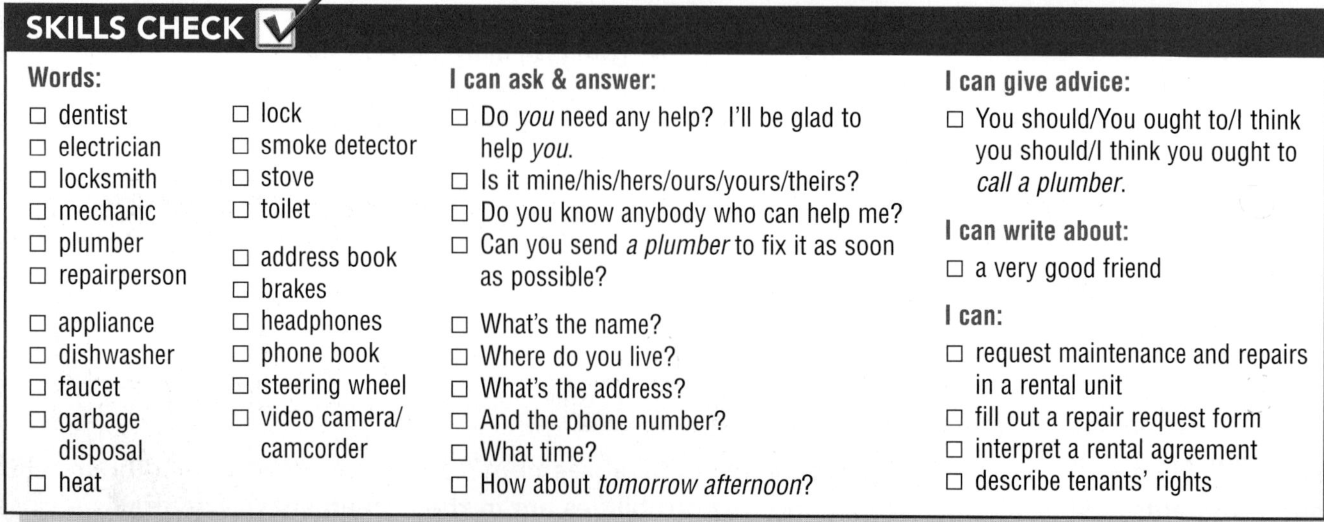

SKILLS CHECK

Words:

- ☐ dentist
- ☐ electrician
- ☐ locksmith
- ☐ mechanic
- ☐ plumber
- ☐ repairperson

- ☐ appliance
- ☐ dishwasher
- ☐ faucet
- ☐ garbage disposal
- ☐ heat

- ☐ lock
- ☐ smoke detector
- ☐ stove
- ☐ toilet

- ☐ address book
- ☐ brakes
- ☐ headphones
- ☐ phone book
- ☐ steering wheel
- ☐ video camera/camcorder

I can ask & answer:

- ☐ Do *you* need any help? I'll be glad to help *you*.
- ☐ Is it mine/his/hers/ours/yours/theirs?
- ☐ Do you know anybody who can help me?
- ☐ Can you send *a plumber* to fix it as soon as possible?

- ☐ What's the name?
- ☐ Where do you live?
- ☐ What's the address?
- ☐ And the phone number?
- ☐ What time?
- ☐ How about *tomorrow afternoon*?

I can give advice:

- ☐ You should/You ought to/I think you should/I think you ought to *call a plumber.*

I can write about:

- ☐ a very good friend

I can:

- ☐ request maintenance and repairs in a rental unit
- ☐ fill out a repair request form
- ☐ interpret a rental agreement
- ☐ describe tenants' rights

![SIDE by SIDE Gazette]

Volume 2 Number 5

Communities

Some communities are friendly, and some aren't

There are many different kinds of communities around the world. Communities can be urban (in a city), suburban (near a city), or rural (in the countryside, far from a city).

Urban communities usually have many neighborhoods, where people often live close together in apartment buildings or small houses. Streets in these neighborhoods often have lots of people and many stores and businesses. People in urban neighborhoods often walk or take public transportation to get to places.

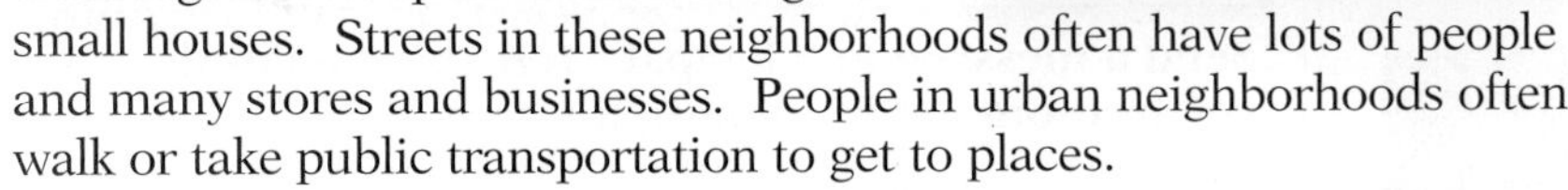

In suburban communities, people typically live in separate houses. Stores and businesses are not usually nearby, and people often have to drive to get there. Some suburban communities have public transportation, and others don't.

In rural communities, people often live far apart from each other, not in neighborhoods. There isn't usually any public transportation, and people have to drive everywhere.

Whether in urban, suburban, or rural areas, some communities are friendly, and others aren't. For example, in some communities, people know their neighbors, they help each other, and their children play together all the time. In other communities, people keep to themselves and sometimes don't even know their neighbors' names.

In the old days, most people around the world lived in small towns and villages, where they knew their neighbors. These days, more people live in large urban communities. Experts predict that in the future most people will live in "megacities" of more than ten million people. Will there be friendly neighborhoods in these communities of the future? Time will tell.

Describe your community. Is it urban, suburban, or rural? Is it friendly? In your opinion, what will your community be like in the future?

BUILD YOUR VOCABULARY!

Household Repair People

A. Who's at the door?
B. The ________ .

appliance repairperson

cable TV installer

chimneysweep

exterminator

house painter

TV repairperson

FACT FILE

The Ten Largest Cities in the World: 1950 and 2010 (Population in Millions)

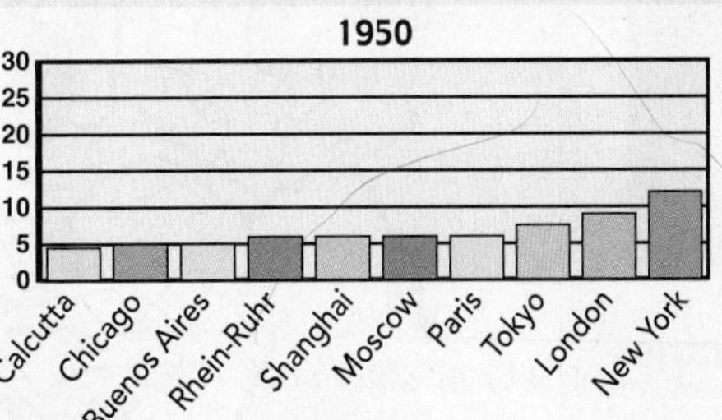

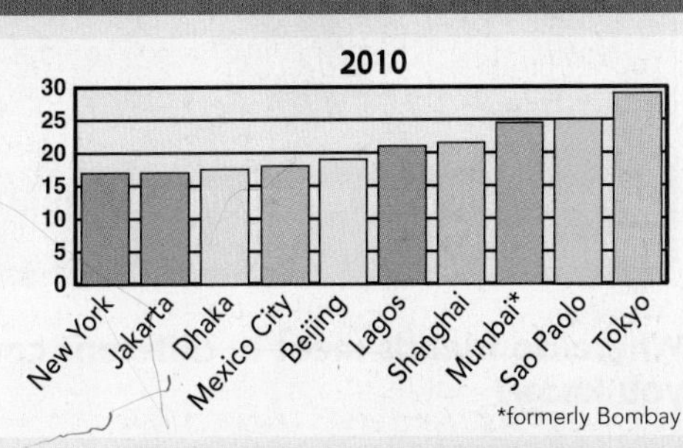

*formerly Bombay

AROUND THE WORLD

Where Friends Get Together

These friends are meeting in the plaza in the center of Guanajuato, Mexico.

These friends are meeting at a coffee shop in Los Angeles.

These friends are talking in a park in Shanghai.

Where do friends meet in different countries you know?

Global Exchange

JuanR: I'm really looking forward to next weekend. Our family will be celebrating my grandparents' fiftieth wedding anniversary! Everybody in my family will be there—my parents, my brothers and sisters, and all my aunts, uncles, and cousins. We're going to have a big dinner at our home. Then, all the grandchildren will present a play that tells the story of my grandparents' lives together. (I'm going to be my grandfather when he was 20 years old!) We're going to have music and dancing, and we're going to give them a special anniversary present—a book of photographs of our whole family through the years. I'll tell you all about the party in my next message.

Send a message to a keypal. Tell about a family celebration you're looking forward to.

LISTENING

Who Are They Calling?

c	1 Amy Francis	a.	mechanic
___	2 Paul Mendoza	b.	locksmith
___	3 Jim Carney	c.	plumber
___	4 Jennifer Park	d.	electrician
___	5 Ed Green	e.	carpenter

What Are They Saying?

APPENDIX

Listening Scripts

Unit 7 – Page 69

What's the Word?

Listen and choose the word you hear.

1. The clinic is on the right, next to the post office.
2. The library is on the left, across from the park.
3. Walk up Town Road to Main Street.
4. Drive along Fourth Avenue to Station Street.
5. Take the subway to Pond Road.
6. The bus stop is at the corner of Central Avenue and Fifth.
7. Take this bus and get off at Bond Street.

Where Are They?

Where are these people? Listen and choose the correct place.

1. A. Do you want to buy this shirt?
   B. Yes, please.
2. A. Please give me an order of chicken.
   B. An order of chicken? Certainly.
3. A. Shh! Please be quiet! People are reading.
   B. Sorry.
4. A. Can I visit my wife?
   B. Yes. She and the baby are in Room 407.
5. A. How much does one head cost?
   B. A dollar fifty-nine.
6. A. Hmm. Where's our car?
   B. I think it's on the third floor.

Unit 8 – Page 79

Listen and choose the best answer to complete the sentence.

1. If I do my homework carelessly, . . .
2. If Sally doesn't feel better soon, . . .
3. If you sit at your computer for a long time, . . .
4. If I stay up late tonight, . . .
5. If you don't speak loudly, . . .
6. If you don't work hard, . . .

Side by Side Gazette – Page 82

Listen to these announcements at different workplaces. Match the workplace and the word you hear.

Attention, all employees! This is Ms. Barnum, the factory supervisor. There were three accidents in our factory last week. Nobody was hurt badly, but I worry about these accidents. Please try to work more carefully. Thank you for your attention.

Attention, all employees! There is a small fire in the building. Please walk quickly to the nearest exit! Don't run! I repeat: There is a small fire in the building. Please walk quickly to the nearest exit!

May I have your attention, please? The president of our company will visit our office tomorrow. Please dress neatly for her visit. Thank you.

Cut! Okay, everybody! That was good, but you're still singing too softly. Please try to sing more loudly. Okay? Let's try that again.

Attention, please! As you know, the weather is very bad this afternoon, and according to the weather forecast, the storm is going to get worse. Therefore, we are going to close the office early today. All employees can leave at three thirty. Get home safely! See you tomorrow.

Unit 9 – Page 91

Listen to the conversations. What happened to these people? Listen and choose the correct answer.

1. A. How did you do that?
   B. I did it while I was shaving.
2. A. When did it happen?
   B. While I was getting off a bus.
3. A. Why do you think it happened?
   B. It was a very hot day.
4. A. The park isn't as safe as it used to be.
   B. You're right.
5. A. What were they doing?
   B. They were playing outside.
6. A. How did it happen?
   B. He dropped the glass.

Unit 10 – Page 97

Listen and choose the correct answer.

1. I couldn't sit down on the bus.
2. Tony wasn't able to paint his house.
3. Jennifer couldn't find her purse last night.
4. They didn't enjoy the food at the restaurant.
5. Why weren't the plumbers able to fix it?
6. Why couldn't you go to work yesterday?

Side by Side Gazette – Page 104

Listen to the messages on Jim's machine. Match the people and their messages.

You have five messages.

Message One, Friday, 2:15 P.M.: Hi, Jim. This is Pete. I just got your message. I'm sorry I won't be able to help you move to your new apartment tomorrow, but I've got to work overtime. 'Bye. [*beep*]

Message Two, Friday, 3:10 P.M.: Hi, Jim. It's Susie. Sorry I won't be able to help you move tomorrow. I've got to visit my grandparents out of town. Good luck! Talk to you soon. [*beep*]

Message Three, Friday, 3:55 P.M.: Jim? Hi. It's Marty! How are you? I'm not so good. I'm having problems with my car. I have to take it to a mechanic, so I'm afraid I won't be able to help you move. Sorry. Give me a call sometime. Okay? Take care. [*beep*]

Message Four, Friday, 5:48 P.M.: Hello, Jim? It's Judy. You know, I really want to help you move, but I've got to stay home all day tomorrow and wait for the plumber. My kitchen sink is broken, and there's water everywhere! Hope your move goes okay. Sorry I can't help. Let's talk soon. [*beep*]

Message Five, Sunday, 9:29 P.M.: Jim? It's Tom. Gee, I'm really sorry I wasn't able to help you move yesterday. I wasn't feeling well, and I had to stay in bed all day. I'm feeling much better now. Call me. Maybe we can get together soon. [*beep*]

Unit 11 – Page 109

Listen and choose the correct word to complete the sentence.

1. **A.** I had my yearly checkup today.
   B. What did the doctor say?
   A. She said I must eat fewer . . .
2. **A.** I had my annual checkup today.
   B. What did the doctor say?
   A. He said I must eat less . . .
3. **A.** How was your medical checkup?
   B. Okay. The doctor said I must drink less . . .
4. **A.** Did the doctor put you on a diet?
   B. Yes. She said I must eat fewer . . .
5. **A.** I went to my doctor for an examination today.
   B. Oh. What did the doctor say?
   A. He said I must eat less . . .
6. **A.** My doctor put me on a diet today.
   B. Really?
   A. Yes. I must eat fewer . . .

Unit 12 – Page 120

Listen to the messages on Bob's machine. Match the messages.

You have eight messages.

Message Number One: "Hello, Robert. This is Aunt Betty. I'm calling to say hello. Call me back. I'll be home all evening. I'll be ironing my clothes. Talk to you soon. 'Bye." [*beep*]

Message Number Two: "Hi, Bob. This is Melanie. I'm making plans for the weekend. Do you want to do something? Call me when you have a chance. I'll be home all day. I'll be studying for a big test. Talk to you later." [*beep*]

Message Number Three: "Bob? This is Alan. What's up? I'm calling to tell you I won't be able to play tennis with you this Saturday. I'll be attending my cousin's wedding in Dallas. See you soon." [*beep*]

Message Number Four: "Hello, Mr. Kendall. This is Ms. Wong from the State Street Bank. I'm calling about your application for a loan. We need some more information. Please call me at 472-9138. You can call this evening. I'll be working until 8 P.M. Thank you." [*beep*]

Message Number Five: "Hi, Bob. This is Rick. Nancy and I want to invite you over to dinner at our new apartment. Call us back. We'll be home all weekend. We'll be repainting the living room. Bye." [*beep*]

Message Number Six: "Hello, Bob. This is Denise. I got your message last week. Sorry I missed you. Call me back. I'll be home this evening. I'll be paying bills. Take care." [*beep*]

Message Number Seven: "Hello. This is a message for Robert Kendall. I'm calling from Dr. Garcia's office. Dr. Garcia won't be able to see you next month. He'll be visiting hospitals in Russia. Please call so we can change your appointment. Thank you, and have a nice day." [*beep*]

Message Number Eight: "Hello, Bobby? This is Mom. Bobby, are you there? Pick up the phone. I guess you aren't there. Dad and I are thinking of you. How are you? Call us, okay? But don't call this afternoon. We'll be exercising at the health club. Well, talk to you soon, Bobby. 'Bye." [*beep*]

Unit 13 – Page 134

What's the Word?

Listen and choose the word you hear.

1. Do you know him well?
2. I'll be glad to help them.
3. Did you see him today?
4. Yours will be ready at five o'clock.
5. Careful! You might hurt yourselves!
6. We're having trouble with her car.

What Are They Talking About?

Listen and choose what the people are talking about.

1. I'm going to have to call the plumber.
2. It's broken. We won't be able to wash the dishes.
3. I'm upset. I can't watch my favorite program.
4. It doesn't work. I can't call anybody!
5. My mechanic fixed the brakes.

Side by Side Gazette – Page 138

Listen to the messages and conversations. Match the caller with the repairperson.

1. A. Hello. This is Dan, the Drain Man. I'm not here to take your call. Please leave your name, number, and the time you called. Also, please describe the problem. I'll get back to you as soon as possible. Have a great day!
   B. Hello. This is Amy Francis. My number is 355-3729. It's three o'clock Friday afternoon. My kitchen faucet is broken. I can't turn off the water! Please call back as soon as possible. Thank you.
2. A. Hello. This is Helen's Home Repair. If you break it, we can fix it! Nobody is here right now. Leave a message after the beep, and we'll call you back. Thank you.
   B. Hi. This is Paul Mendoza. My front steps are broken, and I need somebody who can fix them. My phone number is 266-0381. Please call back soon. I'm having a party this weekend, and nobody will be able to get into my house! Thank you.
3. A. Hi. This is Kevin's Key Service. Leave a message and I'll call you back. Thanks.
   B. Good morning. My name is Jim Carney. I'm really embarrassed. I just lost my keys while I was jogging, and I can't get into my apartment. I'm calling from my neighbor's apartment across the hall. I live at 44 Wilson Road, Apartment 3B. My neighbor's number is 276-9184. Please call back soon. Thank you.
4. A. Gary's Garage. May I help you?
   B. Yes. I think there's something wrong with my steering wheel.
   A. What's the problem?
   B. It's difficult to turn right, and it's VERY difficult to turn left!
   A. Hmm. That's not good. What's your name?
   B. Jennifer Park.
   A. Phone number?
   B. 836-7275.
   A. Can you be here tomorrow morning at eight?
   B. Yes. That's fine. Thank you.
5. A. Hello. Rita's Repair Company.
   B. Hi. Is this Rita?
   A. No. This is the answering service. May I help you?
   B. Yes. My doorbell is broken. It won't stop ringing!
   A. I can hear that. Your name, please?
   B. Ed Green.
   A. Address?
   B. 2219 High Street.
   A. And your phone number?
   B. 923-4187.
   A. Will someone be home all day?
   B. Yes. I'll be here.
   A. Okay. Rita will be there before 5 P.M.
   B. Thank you.

Vocabulary List

Numbers indicate the pages on which the words first appear.

Actions and Activities

add **114c**
agree **72**
answer **81**
apologize **124a**
apply **80c**
apply in person **80c**
argue **128**
arrive **70b**
ask **65**
attach **70c**
attend **92d**
avoid **92b**
baby-sit **96**
bake **70d**
bark **128**
bathe **115**
begin **92b**
believe **68**
bite **83**
borrow **115**
break **79**
break into **83**
breathe **92a**
broil **114c**
buy **78**
call **70a**
call in sick **114d**
cause **70c**
celebrate **124**
change **70a**
charge **102c**
chat online **122**
check (v) **124c**
choke **92b**
clean (v) **70c**
clean out **115**
close (v) **70a**
comb (v) **81**
come **80b**
come in **106**
come home **103**
come over **100**
communicate **82**
complain **128**
complete (v) **80c**
contact **92b**
contain **92c**
contribute **80e**
cook (v) **85**
cool (v) **92b**
cost (v) **136c**
cover (v) **92b**
crash (v) **101**
crash into **83**
cross (v) **70b**
cry **79**
cut (v) **83**
decide **92b**
deduct **136c**
deliver **89**
deposit (v) **136b**
describe **81**
dial **92a**
disconnect **102c**
disturb **102c**
do **76**
do homework **77**
draw **69**
dress (v) **74**
drink (v) **70c**
drip **136a**
drive **64**
drop **83**
drop to your knees **92c**
duck (v) **92c**
eat **70c**
end (v) **136b**
enjoy **96**
enjoy *myself* **96**
enter **70b**
erase **136b**
evacuate **92c**
evict **78**
examine **106**
express interest **81**
faint **83**
fall (v) **79**
fall asleep **128**
feed **126**
feel **76**
file (v) **75**
fill **92c**
find **79**
finish **80f**
fire (v) **78**
fix **85**
flood (v) **135**
flush **136a**
fly (v) **99**
follow **68**
follow the rules **136c**
follow up **136c**
fry **114c**
get down **92c**
get dressed **126**
get into **94**
get off **66**
get on **83**
get out of **83**
get stuck **136a**
get to **62**
get up **74**
give **67**
give advice **113**
go **80b**
go to bed **77**
go back **79**
go to college **121**
go to school **91**
go to work **80**
go up and down **133**
grill (v) **114c**
grow up **124d**
hand in **101**
hang **102c**
happen **70c**
have **76**
have children **121**
hear **79**
help (v) **69**
hire **81**
hold on **120**
hook up **99**
hope **97**
hurry **66**
hurt **70c**
include **102a**
inspect **136b**
install **80a**
invite **69**
iron (v) **115**
itch (v) **79**
keep **70c**
keep clear **102c**
keep out of reach **92b**
knit **115**
know **67**
know how **92a**
last (v) **110**
laugh **79**
lead **106**
leak **136a**
learn **81**
leave **70b**
lift **95**
light (v) **136a**
like **67**
listen **77**
live **69**
locate **124c**
lock (v) **102c**
look **70a**
look for **102c**
look forward to **123**
lose **77**
lose time **80e**
lose weight **111**
mail (v) **70a**
make **70b**
make a list **102a**
make mistakes **77**
make plans **123**
make sure **70c**
measure **106**
microwave **114c**
mop (v) **115**
move **80c**
move out **136b**
name (v) **76**
need **70c**
need to **99**
open (v) **70a**
operate **80c**
order (v) **124c**
overdose **92a**
oversleep **78**

Ailments, Symptoms, and Injuries

Animals, Birds, and Insects

Banking

Clothing

Colors

Community/Civics

Computers

Days of the Week 70a

Department Store/Shopping

Describing Feelings and Emotions

Describing People and Things

Geography

Getting Around Town

Household Fixtures, Home Furnishings, and Appliances

Housing

Meals

Medical Checkup and Medical Care

Medicine

Miscellaneous Nouns

Money

Months of the Year

Nutrition

Objects

Occupations

Parts of the Body

Paycheck 80d

People

Personal Information

Places in the Community

Recreation Activities

School/Education

Sports and Recreation

Telephone

Time Expressions

Transportation

Weather

Work

Work Skills

Cardinal Numbers

1	one	20	twenty
2	two	21	twenty-one
3	three	22	twenty-two
4	four	.	.
5	five	.	.
6	six	29	twenty-nine
7	seven	30	thirty
8	eight	40	forty
9	nine	50	fifty
10	ten	60	sixty
11	eleven	70	seventy
12	twelve	80	eighty
13	thirteen	90	ninety
14	fourteen		
15	fifteen	100	one hundred
16	sixteen	200	two hundred
17	seventeen	300	three hundred
18	eighteen	.	.
19	nineteen	.	.
		900	nine hundred
		1,000	one thousand
		2,000	two thousand
		3,000	three thousand
		.	.
		10,000	ten thousand
		100,000	one hundred thousand
		1,000,000	one million

Ordinal Numbers

1st	first	20th	twentieth
2nd	second	21st	twenty-first
3rd	third	22nd	twenty-second
4th	fourth	.	.
5th	fifth	.	.
6th	sixth	29th	twenty-ninth
7th	seventh	30th	thirtieth
8th	eighth	40th	fortieth
9th	ninth	50th	fiftieth
10th	tenth	60th	sixtieth
11th	eleventh	70th	seventieth
12th	twelfth	80th	eightieth
13th	thirteenth	90th	ninetieth
14th	fourteenth		
15th	fifteenth	100th	one hundredth
16th	sixteenth	1,000th	one thousandth
17th	seventeenth	1,000,000th	one millionth
18th	eighteenth		
19th	nineteenth		

How to Read a Date

June 9, 1941 = "June ninth, nineteen forty-one"

November 16, 2010 = "November sixteenth, two thousand ten" *or* "November sixteenth, two thousand and ten"

Irregular Verbs: Past Tense

be	was	lead	led
become	became	leave	left
begin	began	lend	lent
bite	bit	lose	lost
break	broke	make	made
build	built	meet	met
buy	bought	put	put
catch	caught	read	read
come	came	ride	rode
cost	cost	run	ran
cut	cut	say	said
do	did	see	saw
drink	drank	sell	sold
drive	drove	send	sent
eat	ate	shake	shook
fall	fell	sing	sang
feed	fed	sit	sat
feel	felt	sleep	slept
find	found	speak	spoke
fly	flew	spend	spent
forget	forgot	stand	stood
get	got	steal	stole
give	gave	swim	swam
go	went	take	took
grow	grew	teach	taught
have	had	tell	told
hear	heard	think	thought
hurt	hurt	understand	understood
keep	kept	wear	wore
know	knew	write	wrote

Skill Index

Grammar Index

Topic Index

TECHNOLOGY

TELEPHONE

TIME

TRANSPORTATION

WORKFORCE SKILLS

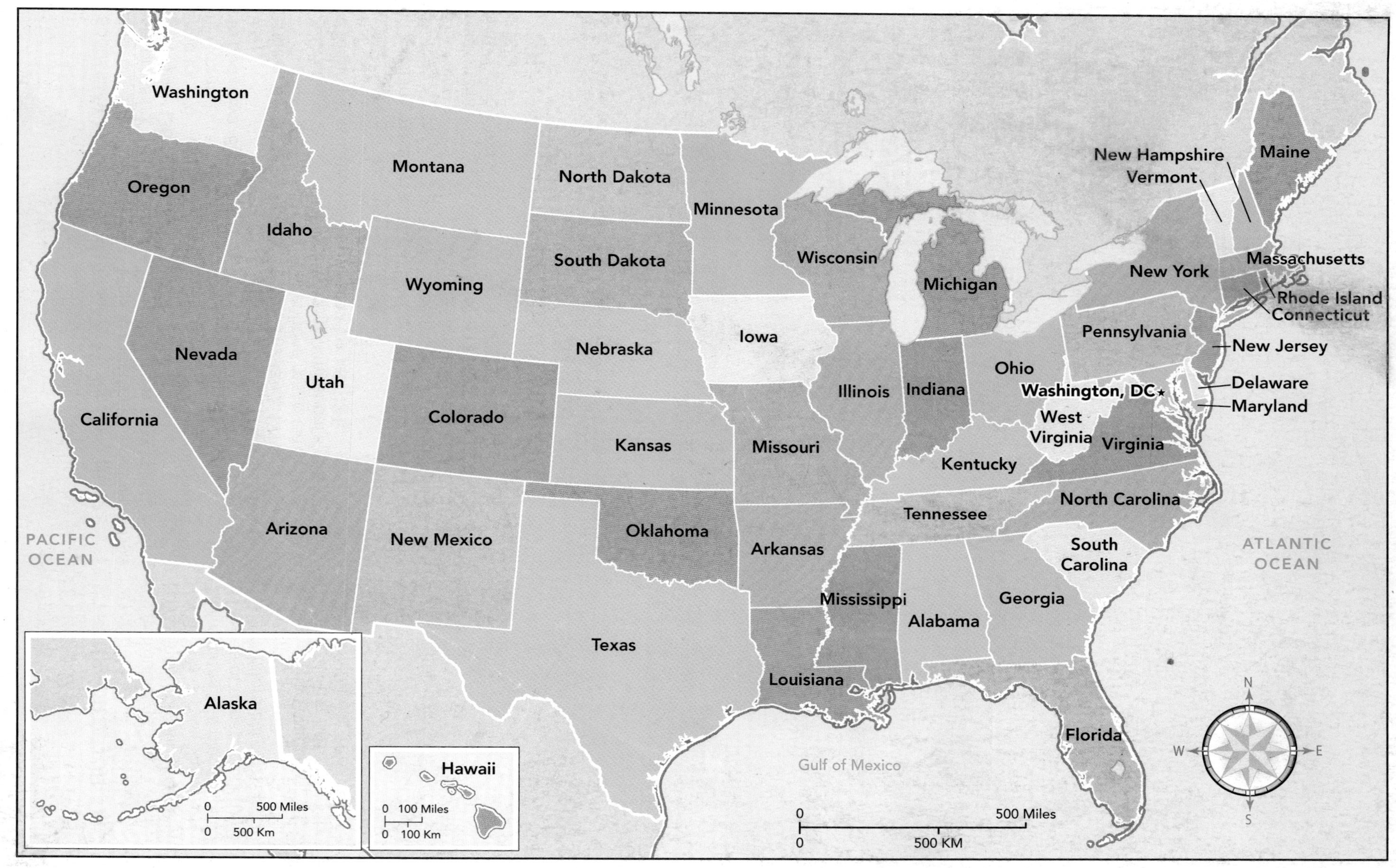

Washington
Oregon
Montana
North Dakota
Minnesota
Idaho
Wisconsin
Michigan
New Hampshire
Vermont
Maine
Massachusetts
New York
Rhode Island
Connecticut
South Dakota
Wyoming
Iowa
Nebraska
Pennsylvania
New Jersey
Nevada
Utah
California
Colorado
Kansas
Missouri
Illinois
Indiana
Ohio
Washington, DC
Delaware
Maryland
West Virginia
Virginia
Kentucky
North Carolina
Tennessee
PACIFIC OCEAN
Arizona
New Mexico
Oklahoma
Arkansas
South Carolina
ATLANTIC OCEAN
Mississippi
Alabama
Georgia
Texas
Louisiana
Alaska
Florida
Hawaii
Gulf of Mexico
N
W
E
S
0 500 Miles
0 500 Km
0 100 Miles
0 100 Km
0 500 Miles
0 500 KM